Swimming Lessons

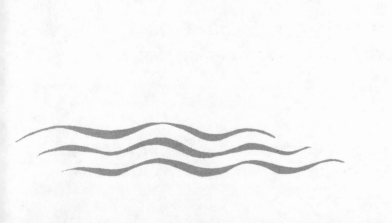

PENELOPE NIVEN

Swimming Lessons

Life Lessons from the Pool,
from Diving in to Treading Water

A HARVEST ORIGINAL / HARCOURT, INC.

Orlando   Austin   New York   San Diego   Toronto   London

www.HarcourtBooks.com

Illustrations copyright © 2004 by Jim Nocito
Excerpt from "The People, Yes" in *The Complete Poems of
Carl Sandburg,* copyright © 1970, 1969 by Lilian Steichen
Sandburg, Trustee, reprinted by permission of Harcourt, Inc.

Library of Congress Cataloging-in-Publication Data
Niven, Penelope.
Swimming lessons: life lessons from the pool, from diving in
to treading water/Penelope Niven.—1st Harvest ed.
p.   cm.—(A Harvest book)
ISBN 0-15-602707-0
1. Women—Conduct of life. 2. Swimming—Miscellanea.
3. Niven, Penelope.   I. Title.
BJ1610.N58   2004
158.1—dc22   2003022047

Text set in Optima
Designed by Linda Lockowitz

Printed in the United States of America
First edition 2004

A C E G I K J H F D B

For my daughter
Jennifer
and
for Barbara
and her daughter
Ella

Contents

Swimming Lessons

Preface

This is not a book about learning to swim. This is a book about learning to live. Swimming Lessons *is written for people of all ages, swimmers and non-swimmers. It is a book about surviving some of the challenges of modern life, and even transcending them. It is also a book about the universal yet personal expedition into "the private seas," as Henry David Thoreau describes the human journey—into "the Atlantic and Pacific Ocean of one's being alone."*

MOST PEOPLE LEARN to swim when they are young. Some people go through life never knowing how to swim at all. Others swallow pride, fear, and a good deal of water in order to learn to swim as adults. I was forty-four when I took my first swimming lessons. They changed my life.

Somewhere during the middle of Swimming Lesson Number Two, I was struck by the profound life lessons embodied in the principles of swimming that I was struggling to learn. For example, before you can swim, you have to enter the water. "Getting in the water is easy," the swimming instructors tell us. "Just walk to the edge and jump in, or slide in, feet first. You can also fall in the water face first, or dive in smoothly with ever-growing confidence and skill."

This premise applies to much more than swimming. Whether you are swimming or beginning a new job, starting a new relationship, writing a first book, getting married, getting divorced, running for office, running a business, bringing up children, or trying to change some aspect of your life, you have no choice but to get in the water. But you do have the power to choose your attitude and your style: Leap in feet first, plunge in face first—or muster the courage to learn how to dive in with grace, confidence, and skill, gathering momentum as you go.

I am a member of what an old friend and I have christened the Drawbridge Generation. (My daughter and her friends, hearing this phrase, insist to the contrary that *theirs* is the Drawbridge Generation. My mother claimed that label for *her* generation.) During every adult life, the world changes dramatically before our eyes and beneath our feet. The great Drawbridge of Change leaves some of us standing perplexed on one shore, some of us thriving or languishing on the other, and some of us hanging on for dear life to the edge of the fast moving bridge. Confronted with many of these changes, most of us do our share of falling into the water face first. Yet we can choose to work awfully hard at learning to dive in with grace and to swim with power and purpose. Swimming is both reality and metaphor throughout these pages. *When you are swimming, you cannot always breathe when you want to. Sometimes you just have to breathe when you can.* This describes the harried days most of us experience in this high maintenance modern world. Sometimes indeed you can't breathe when you want to; you just have to breathe when you can grab a breath. Learning to breathe is crucial in swimming. So is learning to breathe in daily life.

One after another, the lessons I learned in the swimming pool began to resonate in my daily life:

Never dive into waters of inadequate depth. Serious injury is almost a certainty if the water is too shallow.

Be considerate of other swimmers.

Streamline your swimming strokes for simplicity of motion. Wasted or wrong motions result in drag.

Know how to change direction in the water. Turn your body through the water in a wide semi-circle, reaching with your forward arm in the new direction you have chosen. Turn your head in the direction you wish to go, and the rest of your body will follow.

You must learn how to tread water. You must build up your endurance. Treading water can sometimes make the difference between life or death.

Get to know the water where you plan to swim. Look out for hidden dangers below the water that may not be apparent from above or from the shore.

One of your highest goals as a swimmer is to feel at home in the water, and to feel at ease with your ability to handle emergencies.

This book is inspired by these fundamental principles. Each chapter explores a particular metaphorical swimming lesson, drawing examples from experience, observation, and memory, as well as from conversations with people of all ages and backgrounds. The resulting swimming lessons run the spectrum from comedy to tragedy, from farce to triumph, from one life-affirming discovery to another. These swimming principles reverberate in my own life as well as in the lives I witness around me, or read and write about in my work as a biographer.

Diving into shallow water? I realize with a shock that the chief regrets of my life have to do with diving into water too shallow, not into water too deep—with settling for what seemed safe and comfortable instead of stretching toward what seemed difficult or impossible. *Being considerate of other swimmers?* Nothing should be simpler than respecting the rights, the safety, and the dignity of other swimmers. A sailing rule expresses it this way: "You are responsible for your wake." This is the "Do unto others" of the Golden rule of Christian teachings, as well as the religious and ethical teachings of Buddhism, Islam, Hinduism, Judaism, Zorastrianism, and the spiritualism of Native Americans. Yet far too often, we let that basic obligation lapse. Then accidents happen. Conflict happens. On an epic scale, war happens. Tragedy happens.

Wasted or wrong motions result in drag? When you indulge in negative energy or self-defeating behavior, you squander precious breath, emotion, and time—irreplaceable moments of life that can never be retrieved. *Chang-*

ing directions in the water? As a teenager, I innocently assumed that after college I would embark on one sure path that led inevitably to Happily Ever After. It was a surprise to discover that you often have to change directions in the water; that, in fact, you often should; and that you certainly do need to know how.

Treading water? I am not the only person who has had to learn how and when to tread water—to hold on, to wait, to endure—as well as how and when to swim like crazy, with maximum power and speed. *Feeling at home in the water?* How do you recognize and then transcend the hidden dangers of the world you have to navigate? How do you swim safely and even joyfully, despite the risks, and perhaps even because of them? How do you learn to trust the power of the water?

Like life—and swimming—this book is a journey. With each of the ten Swimming Lessons you will find some suggestions for "Swimming Practice": ideas for reflection—for "centering down," as the Quakers say—along with experiments in self-expression. Because I am a writer and a teacher of writing, I encourage you to write in most of these exercises. If you prefer, experiment with other creative ways to adapt these swimming practices to your own needs. Perhaps you will reflect, write, and experiment in a journal or a personal equivalent of a journal: an audio or video recording; a canvas and palette for painting; a camera; the log of a sailboat; or a diary of people you meet, or of stars, birds, wildflowers, and other wonders you encounter in the world around you. There are as many varieties of journals as there are journalists, and as many ways to create a testament to the life you are living, or the life you want to live, as you embark on a deeper personal exploration of the "private seas."

I write also with the hope and conviction that you will discover or rediscover, as I have done, that the oceans are full of fellow swimmers on kindred journeys, all swimming for dear life in search of the enduring shore.

I. Getting in the Water

*Getting in the water is easy: Just walk to the edge
and jump in, or slide in, feet first. You can also fall
in the water face first, or dive in smoothly, with
ever-growing confidence and skill.*

WHEN SHE WAS FOURTEEN and I was forty-four, my daughter, Jennifer, taught me to swim. Jennifer had just finished wearing braces on her teeth, and, thanks to a lower jaw problem, I had just begun. Dire medical necessity, not vanity, mandated that I wear those braces just as I was struggling to cope with menopause, my daughter's puberty, and my husband's midlife crisis. Overwhelmed by these circumstances, I needed diversion, distraction—escape.

I had grown up a swimming illiterate, terrified of the water. Now I was also terrified of wearing braces on my teeth at such a preposterous age, and of seeing my life slip by with some long held dreams unrealized. There was nothing I could do about the braces except endure and survive. But, it occurred to me, I *could* take charge of the dreams.

Many of my dreams had come true, especially my wife and mother dreams, but others haunted me. I had always wanted to write, to travel, to make a lasting, positive difference in the world around me. Some of my more

whimsical dreams were pinned to childhood heroes—
Isaac Stern, for instance. I love music, and, although I play
the piano and the organ, I had dreamed of playing the violin like Isaac Stern. Then there was the Ginger Rogers
dream. I have danced the cha-cha, the waltz, the Texas
two-step, and the jitterbug, but I had always dreamed of
swirling across a stage like Ginger Rogers, ballroom dancing, ballet dancing, tap dancing, even clog dancing my
way to the stars. And I used to dream of swimming like Esther Williams, "The world's most famous and glamorous
swimming star," as she was described on the cover of her
1957 book, *Get in the Swim.* I was a senior in high school
in 1957, not daring to aspire to fame or glamour. I just
wanted to know how to swim so I wouldn't have to sit for-
lornly on the edge of the pool.

People usually learn to swim, tap dance, or play the
violin when they are young. But as I found myself middle-
aged and simultaneously being outfitted with braces and
bifocals, it came to me that I had nothing to lose. I might
as well be twelve again. This could be my chance, perhaps my last chance, to go after some of those childhood
dreams—to learn, however belatedly, to fiddle, tap
dance, and swim. As much as I revered Isaac Stern and
Ginger Rogers, I gravitated toward Esther Williams. I decided to take those long-deferred swimming lessons.

I grew up in Waxhaw, North Carolina, a very small
town where there was no swimming pool. Swimming lessons, if there were any, consisted of being thrown by a

well-meaning parent into a murky pond or into the deep-est pools of Twelve Mile Creek.

"Swim," came the order from the safety of shore. "Now, swim!"

The words echoed in the ears of frightened children as they fought against the mysterious power of the water, si-multaneously learning to fear the water and to distrust the adults in their lives. A child can no more swim on com-mand than she can speak or read or play the violin or stop being afraid of the dark. Nevertheless, countless desperate children have survived that abrupt abandonment to water over their heads. Some swallow fear along with muddy pond water, and muster a clumsy dog paddle in the struggle toward the shore. Some flounder and have to be rescued. Some never get into the water again. Others learn to swim by the book. Still others take to swimming in spite of everything, creating unorthodox breast strokes, swimming ever after with their untutored heads held defi-antly upright in the air.

Fortunately, my parents did not throw me into the languid depths of Twelve Mile Creek or the swampy clutches of Massey's Pond, but neither was I taught to swim in a proper swimming pool, officiated over by trained instructors.

Our family had lived briefly in Charlotte, a city twenty-six miles away, where there were swimming pools aplenty. But there was also the polio epidemic, and for one endless summer we were confined to our dead-end block of Sedgefield Drive with only ourselves and a handful of other children for company. We could see, tantalizingly close, a throng of other children. Their block was longer and there were more children to play with, but we had woods, and they didn't. And all the city swimming pools were closed that summer against the scourge of polio.

Later, we moved back to Waxhaw where I finished elementary school, junior high school, and high school without learning to swim. During my senior year in college, with two other classmates, I spent humiliating hours in the shallow end of the pool at the Greensboro, North Carolina, YWCA, trying to pass the swimming requirement upon which my graduation was conditional. Never mind that I was about to graduate magna cum laude. All that work would count for nothing if I couldn't swim the required distance in the pool. I managed somehow to survive the academic equivalent of being hurled into Twelve Mile Creek.

Paradoxically, I grew up to be a creature who loved water even though I feared it mightily. From childhood I have had a passion for the ocean. Our family spent every summer vacation at the South Carolina shore. During our first summer at Cherry Grove Beach, I jumped waves, holding fast to my father's hand. The salt water transformed my straight brown hair into tangled curls, and my hair has been curly ever since.

More important, from childhood until now, time at the ocean has been essential to the ongoing nourishment of my soul. For even a short time each year, I need to sleep to the rhythm of the sea and climb back into its salty womb in order to recalibrate my interior life. I crave the sensuous, primal energy of the ocean, its vast glory of light and power. I love its deep, briny music and its artifacts: crusty shells; bleached wood; ribbons of seaweed; the warm, limpid pools the tide leaves in the breast of the shore. But I used to regard the ocean with an innate dread, and I did not wade far into its depths. I still go vertically, not horizontally, into the salt water, my feet burrowing into the warm sand at the edge. I love the water lapping at my ankles or breaking at my knees, but terror still overtakes me if I venture by mistake into currents more than waist deep. I am still trying to learn to swim in the ocean.

It was ironic, then, that my husband should have been a sailor, the grandson of a landlocked mountain blacksmith, inheriting from some distant ancestor a manic love for the sea. He had a passion for salty sails, for elegant wooden sailboats heeling almost horizontally into the wind and water of the Chesapeake Bay. I trusted him. If I needed to be rescued from the water I believed I could count on him to see to it. We sailed for many years without mishap.

When Jennifer was old enough, we provided for her aquatic well-being. At the age of three, she started real swimming lessons in a real swimming pool. Before she could read, she was a good swimmer. It was much later, when she was a teenager, that my daughter reciprocated and taught me to swim. When a swimming instructor at the college nearby announced a class for adults who absolutely could not swim and were terrified of the water, I knew my opportunity had come. There were four of us trembling in the shallow end of the Olympic-sized pool for that first lesson. Our instructor was the epitome of patience. He did his best, but soon there were only two of us.

I brought all my latent and conscious fears with me into the shallow water of that pool. You would have thought that I had, indeed, some far distant summer day in Waxhaw, been flung headlong into Twelve Mile Creek or cast to sharks in Massey's Pond. I dreaded each swimming lesson and had to be made to go. Jennifer took my discipline in hand, secretly, I suspect, vindicating every piano lesson, every reluctant day at school, every household chore and doctor's visit I had exacted of her in the fourteen years of her life.

"Maybe it would help if you practice," Jennifer suggested one day. "I'll go with you."

Gratefully, I accompanied my daughter to the pool, urging her to let me stay in the shallow end, where my feet could, on a moment's whim, connect with the reassurance of the concrete floor. Patiently Jennifer coaxed me to demonstrate what I had been trying to learn in the humiliating ordeal of my swimming class. "Floating on my back," I told her in despair. "That's only the first step, and I can't even do that."

"It's almost impossible to sink, Mom," she reassured me.

"That's what you all say," I grumbled. "Ninety-seven percent of people can float. I happen to be one of the 3 percent who can't."

"Of course you can, if you really try and if you really want to," she said with some relish. This was a line I had used with her as she faced new challenges. "Try."

I tried. Arms turning to lead and legs kicking wildly, I foundered and sank to the bottom. Eyes, ears, and nose full of water, I prepared myself to drown. I remember thinking that my death would be much harder on my husband and my child than on me. I wouldn't be around to know about it but they would have to cope with it, call the rest of the family, plan the funeral, and then manage to live without me. It would serve them right. But Jennifer came to the rescue, of course, and insisted that I try again. "Back on the horse, Mom. I'll help you, and I'll be right here," she said soothingly.

During the next half hour she eased me into the pool and supported me as I lay on my back. She pulled and pushed me gently through the water until I got the feel of it. Now and then I would jerk my arms or break into a clumsy kick and begin to sink to the bottom again.

"No, Mom," she'd reprove. "Relax. Just give yourself up to the power of the water."

My daughter, always mature for her years, had made one of the most profound observations I have ever heard about swimming or about living: "I don't understand it myself," she said, "but there is this mysterious power in the water. If you fight against it, you sink every time. If you give yourself up to it, it supports you. You have to learn to trust the power of the water."

Instinctively, she understood an ancient metaphor for faith, as well as the metaphysics and the symbolism of water. As long ago as 3000 B.C., the Sumerians discovered that water can heal. In India, as early as 2000 B.C., earth, air, fire, and water were deemed the basic elements of the material universe and the concept spread throughout the world. To religious people since the beginning of time, water has been sacred, in some views the very source of life itself. Three quarters of the earth's vast surface is dominated by oceans, seas, rivers, lakes, creeks, and springs. And always, everywhere, the growing embryo is cradled in the watery womb.

In that intimidating swimming pool, my daughter taught me how to swim and, in the process, how better to live my life. You do have to learn to trust the power of the water, the power that beats in the mysterious heart of life; as philosophers as various as Trismegistus, Giordano Bruno, and Blaise Pascal have said—the power whose center is everywhere. That is the fundamental lesson in swimming, in writing, in loving, in living—probably even in dying.

But before you can fully trust the power of the water, or your own powers in the water, you have to jump in or fall in or dive in. You have to get wet. There has to be a first time.

JUST AS I HAD dabbled my feet in swimming pools and oceans, I dabbled in writing the first three decades of my life. Writing was my oldest dream, spun out of a love of words before I could even read them or shape them with a pencil—the words I heard my elders speak and sing, the words they read to me. I remember how words looked before I could decipher their geometry—black shapes laid out in their tidy mystery on the pages of storybooks, the Methodist hymnal, or the long columns of the daily newspaper. I was a child in those years before public school kindergartens or television, much less *Sesame Street,* that avenue to precocious recognition of the cryptograms of language.

When I was five, I stood between my parents in the Methodist church one Sunday morning, holding my own hymnal and pretending I could read the words of a song I knew by heart. Like the grownups around me, I glanced down at the words and up again. Suddenly, somewhere along about the third verse, I knew with absolute certainty that someday soon, I would be able to read. Then, I told myself, I would become a writer.

After church that day, thrilled with my discovery, I decided I couldn't wait until I started to school. I needed to learn to write *now.* There was no time to waste. I found paper and a pencil and a favorite storybook, and sat down at the kitchen table to teach myself to write the letters of the alphabet. Once I mastered them, I thought, I would be well on my way to being a writer. When my parents saw what I was up to, they listened patiently to my explanation, and began to give me writing lessons. I was enchanted.

We started with my full name: Penelope Ellen Niven. I

am named for my mother's mother, Penelope, and my father's mother, Ellen. It delighted me to learn that my name had eighteen letters, and six of them were E's. E was the letter I could write first, and best, and P came next. (Recently I found the old dictionary the family used during my childhood; boldly inscribed inside its cover is the letter P—awkward and misshapen, but a P, no doubt about it.) My parents taught me block letters, and then I wanted to learn to write cursive script. I was dazzled by my new knowledge. Now I knew these letters—their names and sounds. With my own hands I could write them on paper, unlocking an ancient, mysterious code. Suddenly I could assemble the letters into words on the page, and decipher the words other people had written in the books I loved.

Yet I was in my forties, wearing those braces and struggling in that swimming class, before I made a serious, full-hearted commitment to writing. "How did I get to be this old?" I asked myself. "Just a moment ago I was five, resolving to be a writer. In another moment I'll be eighty, and full of regret, if I don't dive into the writing." I knew too many older people who seemed eaten up with regret. Intimidated by the prospect of a bitter old age, I threw myself into writing. Walked to the edge and jumped in feet first—scared to death to do it, but more afraid not to. Fell in the water face first more than once, and came up spluttering.

But as time went by, I began to dive in, if not with grace, at least with enough energy and ease so as not to be a danger to myself or others.

It was Carl Sandburg's legendary literary agent, Lucy

Kroll, who proposed that I write a biography of Sandburg. I was intrigued and intimidated. "Oh, I couldn't possibly," I protested. "I don't know how. I've never written a biography." Even before I tested the water, I told myself no.

In appearance and attitude, Lucy was part Tallulah Bankhead, part Bette Davis, and part Queen Victoria. Her words changed my life: "Darling," she said adamantly. "Every biographer has had to write a *first* biography."

That logic cannot be denied whether you are writing or swimming or beginning the first job, making the first speech, plowing the first field, getting the first driver's license, painting the first watercolor, cooking the first meal, designing the first house, becoming a spouse, becoming a parent, or becoming your real self. Every meaningful act must be performed the first time. And sometimes you just have to fall into the water face first, or jump in, tentatively, feet first, or simply slide in, bottom first. At the outset you are likely to be awkward and afraid. In any endeavor, grace, skill, and confidence come later, with hard work and practice.

"What is it you have dreamed of doing?" Lucy asked me. "What is it you want passionately to do? And why aren't you doing it?" In other words, what is it that keeps you from getting in the water? Make your own list. Often it is "What if I can't? What if I fail?"

Almost paralyzed by my lingering phobia about whether I could write that first book, I confided my doubts to a friend. She pulled a worn sugar packet from her purse and handed it to me. "Read this," she said. On the back of the sugar packet were these words: *It is better to try something and fail than to try nothing and succeed.* I carry that sugar packet advice with me. It reminds me that it is better to get into the water any way at all than to stay safe, dry, and warm—timid and intimidated—on the shore.

The clumsy entry into the water and the first awkward dog paddle help me find my fins and swim. Just as a baby can't skip crawling and go straight to walking, a swimmer can't bypass the fundamental lessons and go straight to the Olympics. Even Esther Williams had to work hard at learning to swim.

And what if I make a fool of myself in the water? A certain amount of splashing and floundering is inevitable and necessary, unless I want to spend all my life stranded on dry land. There are certain flightless birds—the kiwi, the cassowary, the ostrich—that originally possessed the ability to fly and lost it. They evolved in habitats that were largely free of challenge. Most flightless birds lived on islands, isolated in the relative paradise of a predator-free environment. Their wings gradually withered from complacency and disuse; safety and security bred atrophy. The bird that failed to climb into the air lost its capacity to soar. Land bound or water bound, relinquishing the sky, it evolved into another creature all together.

This can happen to people who hold back from the challenge of the water and cling to the safety of the shore.

WHEN JENNIFER WAS a few weeks past two, she began to chant, "Yes, I can, I can do it by myself." This was her daily mantra, directed toward any task or challenge. Her persistent resolve was articulated in positives, not the stereotypical negative of the standard two-year-old. It is significant that she did not say, "*No,* I can do it by myself." She said, "*Yes,* I can, I can do it by myself." That is one key to getting in the water. Ultimately, you have to do it by yourself. You have to affirm your power to do it. Lifeguards and teachers, friends and family, may stand by and hover. But *your* skin feels the shock of the cold water; *your* lungs fight for breath; *your* limbs glide or sink.

Despite all the advice others can give you, when you fall in love, you have to swim the exhilarating, capricious currents of romance your own way.

Despite all the support others can give you, when someone you love leaves you through divorce or death, you have to dive by yourself into the deep cold waters of your own grief and swim your own way to the healing shore. Grief and loss are ultimately endured and healed in your own heart, in the locus of your own spirit.

Despite all the guidance and wisdom others can offer, when you set out in search of your true self, you have to walk the convoluted pathway with your own feet.

Once you get the hang of entering the water, you will probably discover, like Jennifer, that yes, you can, you can do it by yourself. You may even find yourself happily, creatively addicted to the water. The creativity muscles, like the swimming muscles, grow stronger with stretching, with exercise and use. They atrophy with neglect, or the paralysis of timidity and fear.

Lower yourself into the water inch by inch. Fall in. Jump in. Dive in. If need be, ask somebody to push you in. Just come on in. The water's fine.

SWIMMING PRACTICE

Swimming Lesson One:
Getting in the Water

1. Divide a sheet of paper into four columns. In the first column, make a list of five things you have always wanted to learn to do but so far have not learned to do.

In the second column, jot down beside each thing your reasons for not learning to do it.

In the third column, write one of the following sentences, filling in the blanks:

A. I still want to learn to do this because _____.
OR
B. I no longer want to learn to do this because _____.

In the fourth column, beside each thing you still want to learn to do, write down a plan for learning to do it, including a date and place. Then do it.

2. Poet William Wordsworth told us that the child is father of the man. Test that hypothesis by composing a snapshot of yourself as a child, just a brief portrait in words, one or two paragraphs. Then reflect about how your childhood self is—or is not—father of the man or mother of the woman you have become.

3. Make a list of pivotal times in your life when you have told yourself *No,* thus closing a door to a relationship, an event, a job, or an opportunity.

4. Make a list of pivotal times in your life when you have told yourself *Yes,* thus opening a door to a relationship, an event, a job, or an opportunity.

5. Jot down events or circumstances in your life that seemed at the time to be dead-ends or detours, but that actually led you to grow or change or move in a meaningful direction.

6. Don't be afraid of what you don't know. Explore new, even unexpected opportunities for getting in the water: Take a class or read a book in a totally new field, or volunteer in a completely new and different area. Explore programs sponsored by local colleges, churches, or community organizations—and choose topics you know nothing about.

II. Learning to Float

Ninety-seven percent of people do not have to learn how to float. Because the human body is inherently buoyant, floating does not usually have to be taught. As Archimedes said, buoyance is an upward force.

SINCE HIGH SCHOOL DAYS I have been a list maker, mapping out my days, weeks, and months with a chart of duties, obligations, appointments, commitments, goals, deadlines, and promises to keep. As I have grown older, the lists have grown ever longer, more complex, more intimidating. I am not alone. We live in a virtual NASCAR race—spinning round and round a treacherous track at breathtaking speed. All about me I see people rushing frantically through life, stretching day into night, overprogramming every minute, and certainly not always by choice. The economic times we live in and wrestle with can drive us to these extremes.

This mania for time management spills into the lives of our children. Because, for safety reasons, modern babies are discouraged from sleeping on their stomachs, they need regularly scheduled, supervised "tummy time." Toddlers are tightly scheduled in day care, play groups, and classes. Instead of lazy days in the sandbox, small children are whisked off to organized play dates. They go to the kiddy gym, to music and dance classes, and to T-ball and soccer. I'm surprised that there aren't toddler-sized electronic organizers to help small children keep up with their hectic schedules, just as their busy parents juggle car pools, jobs, domestic duties—life. We live in a collective frenzy. Sometimes we just need to float.

Few of us have to learn how to float. We are born knowing. See how children bounce when they walk, how they smile, trust, and hope. Until children learn to believe in their own buoyancy in the swimming pool they often hold on to the hands of a parent or swimming instructor. Once they discover their ability to float, they let go and soon begin to swim on their own. Face down in the supine float or face up in the prone float, beginning swimmers discover the security and exhilaration of buoyancy. They learn the power of breath control: To fill the lungs with air is to enhance and maximize buoyancy. As that expert swimmer Benjamin Franklin observed, "It is not so easy to sink as you imagine. . . . You feel the power of water to support you, and learn to confide in that power."

Buoyancy is an upward force, born in us, as natural to the body as breathing. We learned that from Archimedes, the inventor and mathematician (ca. 287–212 B.C.), and he learned it by chance. Like many explorers and discoverers, he was looking for one thing when he found another, even better thing. It is said by Plutarch and others that King Hiero II of Syracuse asked Archimedes to determine if the goldsmith who had made the monarch's new crown had used pure gold or part alloy. One day, as Archimedes settled into his bath and thought about how to solve the puzzle, he noticed that the water was brim-

ming over, cascading out of the bath. He began to con-
jecture, then to calculate, and then to conclude: A body
immersed in fluid loses weight equal to the weight of the
fluid displaced. The body completely or partially submerged in the water is supported by an upward force
equal to the weight of the fluid the body displaces. He'd
hit upon the principle of buoyancy. Undeterred by the
fact that he had discovered something other than what he
had hoped to discover, Archimedes supposedly leaped
from the tub and ran naked through the streets of Syracuse, crying triumphantly, "Eureka!" ("I have found it!")

Just as the body is inherently buoyant, there can be an
innate buoyancy of heart, mind, and spirit. Unfortunately,
however, other people can squelch and stifle instinctive,
natural buoyancy—joy, trust, and hope. Other people can
stamp it out of us, if we let them. Negative energy can sap
the effervescence of people graced with positive energy.
Some people seem to emit negative energy in the active
or passive effort to override positive energy. There are
people who doubt their own gifts and so belittle the gifts
of others; people who do not love themselves and so cannot love anyone else; people who do not think beyond
their own needs and desires and move through the world
heedless of the rights of others. They are bent on destruc-
tion. They do not honor the inherent buoyancy of the
human spirit. They seek to deny and suppress the innate
upward force of joy and faith. They thrive on the downward forces—selfishness, thoughtlessness, greed, hatred,
pessimism, despair.

There are, of course, people who do not possess natural buoyancy. Through circumstance, choice, or conditions beyond their power, they cannot float. These are people with negative or neutral buoyancy. In swimming this happens most often to adults with limited lung capacity or to heavily muscled men. In life outside the pool, just as in swimming, you can achieve positive buoyancy by wearing a swimming apparatus such as a buoyancy belt. In other words, if you are not born with buoyancy, you may need to find some additional help and support—and it's not only all right to do so, it's smart.

Like runners, swimmers can achieve a state of euphoria. One happy by-product of swimming is that it clears the mind and frees the buoyant spirit, in part, I think, because the swimming body is suspended temporarily in a different relation to gravity. This also happens to me in the hammock, or on an airplane as it soars to its cruising altitude. Swimming has helped me understand what perspective means to the visual artist who works with canvas or camera. Perspective is a key to life. Ever since I began learning how to relax and give myself up to the water—how to float—I have been fascinated with perspective. I know that when I write I need to test and often to change the angle of vision—to stand on my head, if necessary, to look at a biographical figure from many perspectives. Like sleeping or lolling in my hammock, swimming temporarily frees my body from the customary vertical perspectives of life and the physical universe.

One of my favorite swims occurred in a heated out-door pool in the snow in Breckenridge, Colorado. I swam the backstroke with snowflakes licking my face. Snow-flakes dance a different dance when you are flat on your back. Mountains loom even higher. Stars in the night sky shimmer on different planes. With its refreshingly different horizontal angle of vision, floating brings its own clarity.

Floating also brings deep relaxation of muscle and mind. At the end of a swim, I like to float on my back, eyes closed, bobbing like a buoy. Often, I've almost fallen asleep during a mindless, enervating float. Lifeguards or other swimmers have even checked to be sure I was still alive. I have set out on many a swim with chains of per-sonal or professional concerns constricting my mind and spirit: how to begin or end a chapter; how to deal with a difficult business or personal problem; how to cope with the specter of someone else's serious illness or my own; how to endure a broken trust or a broken heart; how to survive in a chaotic world. Time after time I have enjoyed a floating epiphany—my own Eureka moment, like Archi-medes when the bath overflowed. Solutions break through, chapters crystalize, worries fall into proportion and per-spective, and scars begin to heal. A certain period of float-ing is fundamentally necessary to any creative act.

But you don't need a swimming pool or a lake or even an ocean in order to float. Let your mind float: meditate; write in a journal; write wonderful poems or awful poems or both; stretch and breathe, slowly, lazily, indolently.

Daydream. Give in to the upward force, the natural buoyancy. To swim is to *do;* to float is to *be.* Let yourself simply
be. Even for five minutes a day, just be.

AS WE HAVE BEEN TOLD by philosophers and poets (including the poet Helga Sandburg), there are times when
we have to bear the unbearable. How do you float under
overwhelming weight? How do you bear with any grace
what is too hard to be borne? Sudden, shocking deaths.
Prolonged, agonizing deaths. The staggering grief of losing a child, losing a marriage, losing a business, losing a
long-held personal dream, losing national innocence. Do
you thrash furiously, helplessly in the rough waters? Do
you let go, give up, drown? Or do you survive, acquiesc-
ing to something larger, stronger, and more enduring than
yourself? Do you float?

Antoine de Saint-Exupéry recorded in *Wartime Writ-
ings 1939–1944* this conviction: "It is always in the midst,
in the epicenter, of your troubles that you find serenity."
The epicenter of your troubles. Look there for serenity, for
buoyancy. Part of the secret is looking the trouble hard in
the face, head on, eyes unblinking. Do every possible
thing you can do about it, and then do even more—try
the impossible. Then float. Just rest and float and trust the
power of the water.

To be buoyant is to be resilient. We once built a
house on a bluff overlooking the Saint Mary's River in
southern Maryland. From our waterfront windows we
could look down the Saint Mary's to the mouth of the Po-

tomac River. Storms from the Chesapeake Bay often roared up the Potomac to attack our bluff. Ancient, pliable cedar trees cushioned the assault of the gales, but the younger oak trees, rigid in the storm, were no help at all. The rain-swept cedars bent and bowed gracefully in the wind and survived the storms intact. The stubborn oak trees, rigidly defiant, cracked and shattered, their useless limbs dropping to the shore to be bleached like bony shells, or swallowed in the tidal river. Better to be a cedar than an oak, I concluded. There was virtue in resilience. There was survival and continued growth despite the assailing elements.

Once I asked a particularly accomplished, productive woman how on earth she managed to balance all the rigorous demands of her life. "I have great physical energy," she told me. "And I have been blessed with soul stamina." When you have soul stamina the resilient spirit is empowered by the upward force. You can work a lifetime growing soul stamina. One way or another—by attention or neglect—I am responsible for the inward life I live, and for the soul I grow.

"Trust the power of the water," Jennifer told me. This has become our metaphor for spiritual belief. Faith requires work and energy; to keep faith is to dive into the depths, to swim hard, to tread water, and sometimes, just to float. I straddled a seesaw of faith and doubt during some dark days in my life until it finally occurred to me that anybody can be faithful to any belief system when everything goes well. Faith is a cinch when the going is good. Like the magnitude of an earthquake, the true measure of faith is taken in the epicenter of trouble. I had been fighting in vain to swim against the current of rough waters. I was exhausted, and I had lost my bearings. It was time to give myself up to the power of the water—to float, cradled by the invisible force that supports weary bone, muscle, tissue, and corpuscle in the water. To float supported by the invisible force that cradles the spirit in the mysterious choreography of life, struggle, transcendence, and death.

Henry David Thoreau said, "I did not wish to live what was not life, living is so dear." That stunning recognition gives rise to buoyancy, resilience, joy, hope, faith. Living is so dear—in spite of and because of illness, misfortune, loss, death, or catastrophe. Joy comes readily and faith is easy to hold onto when times are good. Learning to float has taught me that I can re-find joy. I can hold to faith in the epicenter of trouble if I trust the power of the water. Whatever your vocabulary of spiritual belief, your geography of faith, buoyancy is undergirded by some innate, almost primal life force—spirit, love, hope.

Calibration of the spirit relies on discovery of the God within, as the Quakers say, and on alignment with the Something or Someone Beyond. In individual and common voyages of spiritual discovery, there are many names for the Power of the Water. The point is to embark on the voyage, to be open to the discoveries, and to trust the upward force that supports the smallest ships on the vast open sea.

When Jennifer was seven going on eight, she began to

doubt the existence of Santa Claus. She had been set upon by the inevitable cynics in her second grade class, little know-it-alls who sabotaged the childhood beliefs of their more trusting classmates. It was nearing Easter time when Jennifer came to me and said gravely, "Tell me the truth about Santa Claus."

Her father and I had planned our response, so I was reasonably well prepared for the talk. I emphasized the loving mythology involved, and the unselfish joy parents take in fulfilling their children's hopes and wishes while Santa Claus gets all the credit. Jennifer listened soberly, nodding at key points.

"I'm not surprised," she said at last. "I couldn't see how Santa Claus could pack all those toys into his sleigh and get up and down all those chimneys and know where every boy and girl might be and get all around the world so fast, even if there are different time zones. And I couldn't understand why some children got left out."

She paused and thought about it for a moment longer, and then she said, with a deep sigh of relief, "Well, thank goodness we still have the Easter bunny!"

Faith often involves what poet Samuel Taylor Coleridge called the willing suspension of disbelief: Sometimes you have to relinquish your faith in Santa while you still maintain your faith in the Easter bunny. At the end of one of his books, Dr. George Crile quoted the unknown writer who said, "Death is a horizon, and what is a horizon but the limit of our sight?" Faith goes far beyond the limit of sight and the boundaries of rational thought.

In order to float we entrust ourselves to the power of the water. We have to believe in what we cannot see and give ourselves to what we cannot fully comprehend. But as surely as gravity anchors us to the earth beneath our feet, buoyancy is an upward force, thrusting us toward the air and the light. To trust the power of the water is to swim or float buoyed by the sure, surging strength of the upward force.

SWIMMING PRACTICE

Swimming Lesson Two:
Learning to Float

1. Make an energy inventory, listing the people and activities giving you buoyancy, or positive energy. Then make a list of the people and activities in your life draining your buoyancy and generating negative energy. Next, analyze your lists to see how you can increase the positive energy and minimize the negative energy.

2. For three days out of the next seven, treat yourself to at least twenty minutes each day just to be—to float, literally or symbolically. Lie down on the sofa or on the floor or in the hammock. Stretch and breathe. Daydream. Meditate. Do nothing at all. Let yourself simply *be.* Work toward giving yourself at least ten or fifteen minutes of floating time every day.

3. Divide a sheet of paper into three columns. In the first column, make a list of two or three problems that are worrying you, skipping several lines between each problem. In the second column, make a list of possible solutions to each problem. In the third column, make a list of ideal but seemingly impossible solutions to each problem. Don't edit yourself as you make this list. Jot down ideal solutions even if they seem preposterous and impossible. Sometimes this juxtaposition of the probable with the improbable will produce just the answer you are seeking. If a solution emerges, act on it. If not, seal the sheet of paper in an envelope. Return to it in a week. Reassess the problem. Search again for the solution.

4. It is probably impossible to condense a spiritual credo into one paragraph, but give it a try. Write a paragraph beginning, "I believe in _____."

Then write a paragraph beginning, "I do not believe in _____."

III. Propulsion

All forward motion depends on pulling or pushing the water while your body is floating. Because floating requires little effort, you can put all of your energy into your arms and/or legs. They can pull or push the water as vigorously or as gently as you choose.

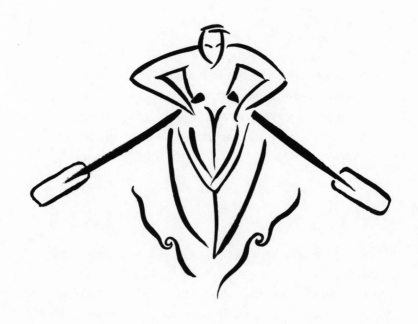

YOU HAVE FOUND YOUR buoyance and you trust the power of the water sufficiently to float. You can now pour all your energy into forward motion, propelling yourself onward as vigorously or as gently as you choose at any given moment, except, of course, for those moments when the waters are choppy, the current is running strongly against you, and you are buffeted by the wind.

In his Third Law of Motion, the English mathematician and physicist, Sir Isaac Newton, deduced a principle that swimmers need to bear in mind: "For every action, there is an equal and opposite reaction." I fight against the water. I sink. I relax in the water. I float. I direct my energy in certain ways and I achieve propulsion—onward, forward motion. Progress. Growth. I direct my energy in other ways and I move backward.

A major goal in swimming is propulsion—onward, forward motion. If I want to propel myself forward in the water, I have to push the water backward. Stretching my arms, sculling with my hands, kicking with my legs and feet, I must move the water of the past backward if I want to move into the present and go forward into the future.

You see swimmers doing this all around you: the baby climbing off her knees and learning to walk; the child bent on learning to skate, toppling to the sidewalk, brushing off the pain, and getting up to try again; the young man or woman tackling the first job; parents hovering over a new baby; the man or woman at midcareer, laid off or let go, mustering the grit and courage to start over again; the elderly person relinquishing a longtime home because health and changing circumstances demand a new way of living; a community rebuilding after a flood, giving up what was to build what can be. Vigorously or gently, we can invest our energy in propulsion, and harness it for growth, for progress.

But this is not always as easy as it sounds. Let us say you have suffered an earth-shattering, unforgettable, undeserved disappointment. You are aggrieved. Someone has broken your heart. You have been unfairly used in your professional life, or betrayed by someone you loved or trusted in your personal life. The water is littered with the debris of the damage done. You are floating in all the flotsam and jetsam of the disappointments in your life. Are you going to remain there, hobbled by the wreckage? Or is it forward motion you are after? You can choose to stay mired in that whirlpool—or you can move on.

FOURTEEN YEARS AGO, as I was struggling upstream after the end of my long marriage, I lost my buoyancy. I foundered until I beached. For a long blur of time—days?—weeks?—I was immobilized by deep grief and, worse, a profound conviction of failure. After I was finally resettled in a new home in a new city, I spent days lying morosely on the sofa listening to Beethoven. Never mind that I had a beautiful young adult daughter to nurture and enjoy, even though she was a freshman in a university many miles away. Never mind that, at last, I had a contract to write my first book. Never mind that I was surrounded by a strong, loving family and strong, loving friends. I was nearly fifty. I believed I had failed as a wife and, therefore, as a woman. My life was over.

It did not occur to me at the time that I was depressed. One day I finally forced myself to get up and go to the YMCA swimming pool and jump into the water and swim. I remember very little from my brief collegiate encounter with physics, but as I swam that day my thoughts drifted to what I understood about inertia and momentum. Goodness knows I had been inert for long enough, mired in Beethoven and self-pity. "You need to get yourself some momentum, girl," I urged myself. "Stay off that sofa. Even if you go the wrong way, go some way."

My mind turned to the swimming lesson that focused on propulsion. "You have the power to propel yourself through the water," my swimming instructor had taught me. There could be no forward motion in my future so long as I moped on that sofa. I could lie there, inert, letting time pass me by. A month of this inertia could easily turn into a year of inertia, even a lifetime of inertia. Or I could get up, move the old water backward, move forward into new water, gather momentum, and propel myself into the future. It was time to hold on to promise and possibility and let go of loss and regret. It was "moving on" time.

But troubles seemed to multiply. The unimaginable had happened to me and kept happening. There was never enough money or time. I stood virtually alone, I thought, at a personal and professional crossroad. There were illnesses in my family. People died. My daughter struggled to make sense of the decisions her parents had made. Her father remarried. I discovered a lump in my breast.

In the epicenter of my troubles, for a time, there was sheer terror. It was not definitively cancer, reported the surgeon who performed the lumpectomy, but he recommended a bilateral mastectomy just in case. I set out in search of other opinions and options, and found them, and honored them. My daily prayer became, "Whatever happens, help me to be able to stand it—and pay for it."

As Jennifer said after one more well-meaning friend told us that trouble builds character, we had built all the character we could stand to build for a while. A person can only build so much character.

My search for that second opinion led me, with the help of Carl Sandburg's daughters, to Dr. George "Barney" Crile of the Cleveland Clinic. Dr. Crile was Helga Sandburg's husband and a pioneer in less radical methods of treating breast cancer. He took over my case, and his pathologists ruled out cancer. Severe hyperplasia was the diagnosis, stimulated by the hormone therapy I'd been on for a few years. Barney took me off the hormones and instructed me to stay off them permanently. He worked out a regimen to monitor my health. Finally, he told me, "Now you get out there and *live* your life. Don't hold back."

"I will," I promised Barney. His words and deeds reenergized me. He enabled me to bounce back to good health, in body and spirit. He encouraged me to reclaim my buoyancy and to propel myself toward a new life.

DIVORCE SMASHES ALL your old dreams of a lifelong marriage. My generation grew up with that model and mandate. You married the one person in all the world who was meant for you. We members of the Drawbridge Generation never imagined ourselves ever being divorced. Like our own parents and the parents we watched on television—the Cleavers, the Nelsons, Donna Reed—we were married for life. After all, most nice girls had saved themselves for marriage, marching down the aisle with dreams, innocence, and virginity intact, to live happily ever after. It was destiny. It was duty. It was forever. It never occurred to us that we might fail.

Then our world changed. John Kennedy was the first president of our adulthood, and our innocence died with him that November day in 1963. Any vestiges of our hope and trust perished with the assassinations of Dr. Martin Luther King, Jr., and Robert Kennedy in 1968. Vietnam was the first war of our adulthood, and we are still trying to figure out what it did to us, no matter where our consciences and our bodies wound up during the tortured duration of that "conflict." As adults, we have had to cope with the 1970s, the '80s, the '90s, and then the first rough years of the new Millennium. Did external events help to convert us into the first generation in history to divorce each other in unprecedented numbers? How did this happen?

AFTER YEARS OF WORK and thought, I realized that divorce can sometimes be a necessary act, even an act of courage. Now, as I look around me, I see almost as many healthy divorces as I see healthy marriages. Some marriages fail, some wear out, and some even do harm. But some marriages simply *culminate.* When life expectancies were far shorter than they are now, the typical marriage had a shorter life span. There was a time when a quarter century of marriage was a remarkable feat, for, long before couples reached that anniversary, women could die in childbirth, or either partner could succumb to old age. These days it is not uncommon for people to divorce after twenty, twenty-five, or thirty or more years of marriage. Setting aside the occasional displacement of an older spouse for a younger, trophy spouse, some marriages may simply culminate. The work of that marriage has been accomplished. The marriage has run its course.

No matter the cause, however, divorce is death with a capital D. Hopes, faith, and dreams die long before love dies. A marriage can die a slow, sometimes invisible death, a civil, steady, imperceptible slipping away. But there is no funeral. Nobody brings you casseroles. For a time the buoyancy is gone, but you've still got to float and, if possible, to propel yourself forward.

But bouncing back from the heartbreak of divorce can take some doing. Some people become spouses again right away, some people become serial daters, and some people become hermits, reclusively protecting battered hearts and egos. I was a hermit for a good long while, until someone I had known and trusted most of my life lured me out of my cave. Then came more heartbreak. Back to the cave. But along came a sweet, handsome, good-hearted, much younger man. A tonic for the heart, soul, and ego. Both of us recognized this relationship for what it was—a lovely detour on the great highway of life. But he taught me a wonderful lesson in that short time. "I may not be Mr. Right," he told me. "But I can be Mr. Right Now."

I'll always be grateful to Sir Isaac Newton, Dr. Barney Crile, and Mr. Right Now for pulling me out of the cave into the sunlight. For reminding me to shed the past and reach for the future. For urging me to savor the Now—not to lose Today because I'm hiding behind Yesterday, or holding back from Tomorrow.

HAVEN'T WE ALL lived through those "moving on" events after circumstance clobbers us? A relationship ends. A job is lost. An illness is diagnosed. A disappointment knocks the joy and the hope out of us. Worries weigh us down so we can hardly walk, much less swim. My swimming lessons have led me to this formula for moving on:

1. Learn the lesson in the experience.

2. Let go of every possible burden from the past, especially the obsolete burdens.

3. Stow in the swimming locker the burdens you must carry.

First, learn the lesson in the experience. Identify the paradoxical gift, for hidden somewhere in the experience, no matter how bitter, there is a gift, no matter how small. Thornton Wilder wrote, "By a strange spiritual law positive personalities so far assimilate their lives that they would not wish their very misfortunes otherwise. Their destiny is themselves." My destiny is, or should be, my fullest, truest self. How can I assimilate my misfortunes into a deepening richness of life? How can I convert painful lessons into wisdom?

Do I regret my marriage? Never for a moment. It was itself a wondrous gift, and it yielded abiding gifts too numerous to count—greatest among them Jennifer.

Is there profound unhappiness in divorce? Of course. I resolved early on to make a timely peace with my divorce. I knew people who were clinging to their anger, pain, and regret years after divorce. Bitterness can destroy beauty and implode—fracturing any hope of serenity, peace, joy. I have known people who have clung to anger for a lifetime. A woman harbors the bitterness of betrayal in her marriage, punishing her husband and herself year after year. A father holds on to his disappointment in a son. A man begrudges the family responsibilities that he believes have kept him from his dreams of being an artist. A woman resents the shortcomings and failures of her parents long after they are dead. In all these cases, unresolved bitterness festers and grows, infecting everything it touches. Eventually there is no room for anything else, and bitterness displaces buoyancy. It stands in the way of growth. There is no forward motion, only swimming backward, mired in the past.

Yesterday is gone. I have to push the water back if I want to swim forward. Newton's Law. Simple as that. I have to let go of the past and reach for the now, reach for the future. As a wise priest put it, you have to die to certain realities in order to be born into the new. Die to the old hatreds, the old disappointments, and the old regrets. Honor the lessons you have to learn from the past, the memories that nourish you, the experiences, good and bad, that have made you who you are this moment. Let the rest of it go—the detritus of old hurts and shopworn grudges. Shed them like an outgrown skin. Swim forward, clean and unfettered by the drag of the past.

How do you let go of what must be discarded? Ventilate. Communicate. Eliminate. There is the Serenity Prayer: "God, grant me the serenity to accept the things I cannot change, courage to change the things I can, and wisdom to know the difference." There is your own private version and vocabulary of prayer. There is counseling therapy. Jennifer was a remarkably sweet-tempered little girl, but on those rare times that she was angry and words didn't work, we encouraged her to use a punching pillow to ventilate. Later, I learned there is a similar method in Primal Therapy.

You can meditate. Exercise. Make peace before sunset. Write what Abraham Lincoln called Hot Stove Letters. He wrote these letters to people who had sparked his temper or wounded his feelings. He transferred his pain or anger to paper and then burned the letter in a hot stove. On occasion, he held on to a letter and tucked it into the lining of his stovepipe hat. Carl Sandburg, a biographer of Lincoln, adopted this habit, although he wore a fedora or a golfer's cap instead. I decided to borrow Sandburg's therapy, borrowed from Lincoln—and it works every time. I encourage my fellow writers to try it. Write a letter to the person who has hurt you. Pour out your feelings. Hold nothing back. Put all of it on paper, every angry, bitter, painful word. Write down the reasons for your pain and anger. Spill out everything you'd like this person to know about the harm inflicted on you. Ventilate. Purge. No holds barred. Get it all out of you onto the waiting page. But don't send the letter. The act of writing it is cathartic, cleansing, and liberating.

Of course some worries inevitably stay. There is still a living to be earned. People you love get sick and die. Accidents happen. Troubles come. The world careens in directions that disturb you deeply—and what difference can one person make? What do you do with the perennial worries, the problems that wait to be solved, the problems that can't be solved? Learn the constructive art of Checking the Baggage.

In our family, some of us are overly endowed with what we call the Packing Gene. We set out on journeys—long or short—laden with baggage. On a recent four-day trip to spend Thanksgiving with my daughter and son-in-law, I took one large pocketbook, two suitcases, one brief case, one tote bag, two garment bags, four shopping bags, and a large cooler. When I go swimming, I take my purse and a large swimming bag bursting with items I consider essential for preparing to swim, swimming, showering after swimming, and dressing to go home after swimming. I would not think of setting off on a trip or a swim without all my stuff. But I certainly would not think of carrying all my stuff every moment I am traveling or swimming. I load my luggage and shopping bags and cooler in the car. I lock my swimming gear in the locker in the dressing room.

You don't have to carry all of your baggage all of the time. You can't. If you spend all your energy hauling the baggage around, you'll be too exhausted to move forward, or even to float. Check the baggage. Compartmentalize. Leave the stuff you have to carry in the locker when you can't carry it, don't have to carry it, or can't attend to it. I can't swim and, at the same time, carry my towel, my clothes, my shampoo, my hair dryer, and my car keys. I can't write with all my mind and heart and, at the same time, focus on my concerns about my parents' health; my daughter's grief over her father's death; my grief over his death; my brother's ongoing recovery from a stroke; my students' struggles to get into graduate school, get published, get jobs; and my world's struggle for peace, prosperity, justice, survival. When I write, I write—focusing on that act as if it were all in the world I had to do. (The biographer Robert Caro advocates sitting down to write and saying, "There is nothing in the world but this blank page.") When I swim, I swim. I entrust the other endeavors of my life to the safety of the locker.

Then, deeply restored and reinvigorated by the writing or the swimming, I open the lockers one at a time. I try to remove the contents—the project, the concern, the problem, the responsibility—item by item. I give that one thing my full attention, do all I can do about it, and return it to the locker until next time. Otherwise, I am overwhelmed. Instead of floating, I jeopardize my buoyancy and my power to move forward.

One of Jennifer's friends, aware that Jennifer was working night and day to finish a book, all the while coping with her father's terminal illness, said sympathetically, "Jennifer, you look like a beautiful swan gliding serenely on the surface of the pond—but underneath, I know you are paddling like hell." Most of us experience those swan moments when we appear to be gliding but we are actually paddling like hell. I also have moments when I am gliding in circles, making no progress in any direction. It feels as if I am trapped in one of those nightmare traffic circles, going round and round trying desperately to make the proper turn, or any turn at all. Sometimes—in my swan moments—I seem to be paddling backwards. It is forward motion we are after here. Propulsion.

I've come to see that I can achieve forward motion in small increments—in my private life, in my swimming life, and in my writing life. I signed my first book contract in 1985, when I was 46. The book, *Carl Sandburg: A Biography,* was published in 1991. It was written—all 843 pages of it—in what I call patchwork quilt scraps of time. Most of us have jobs to be done, families to be cared for, duties to be fulfilled. Very few writers in history have ever enjoyed total time and freedom to write. William Shakespeare, after all, was writing next week's play while he was acting and producing. Nathaniel Hawthorne had to work in the Boston customhouse. Herman Melville worked as a seaman and, for nearly twenty years, as a customs inspector on the docks of New York City. You could find Willa Cather and Carl Sandburg working in newsrooms; the Brontë sisters in schoolrooms; T. S. Eliot in a bank; and Wallace Stevens in an insurance company. Nowadays—except for an extraordinarily successful few—writing full time seems an impossibility unless your book gets wide television exposure or you get sent off to prison.

MOST OF US HAVE TO write against the grain of time, in the middle of busy days and nights, in hour long scraps of time, or less. Early in the days of work on my first biography, I despaired that I would ever finish. I yearned to spin a continuous thread of time and weave it into the whole blanket of a book, neat and tidy. I could not do that. My family is, was, and will always be my first concern. I was teaching and living an active life in my community. Then I realized in another epiphany that, while I could not make a blanket, I *could* make a quilt—a scrap at a time. The quilt could be as useful as a blanket—and perhaps, I hoped, even more beautiful, vivid, and enduring. The first book and the ones that followed have been written in those prized moments alone—those bright, precious scraps of time. You can do all sorts of things besides write that way. You can propel yourself onward, one swimming stroke at a time.

MY BROTHER BILL, who is one of the most courageous people I have ever known, had a stroke when he was fifty-one. The stroke took away his peripheral vision, twenty-five percent of his visual field, some of his cognitive skills, and all of his short-term memory. It did not take away his sense of humor or his wit, two gifts he inherited from our father. A few days after the stroke, the neurologist in the hospital gave me a list of all the things my brother probably would not be able to do in his post-stroke life—read, write, work, live alone, use his camera. The depressing litany went on and on. I finally interrupted him. "Please," I said. "We are not going to tell Bill what he may not be able to do. If he can't do these things, he will find out for himself all too soon. But maybe he *can* do them; and if we tell him he can't, he may be too discouraged to try."

Since the stroke, Bill has embarked on a brave, even heroic odyssey. He has propelled himself forward through sheer will power and a dogged stubbornness. He has made even better pictures after the stroke than before. Word by word, he has taught himself to read again, devising a way to compensate for the visual field loss, although his memory deficit keeps him from remembering what he reads. He has taught himself how to use a computer again. He has embarked on a spiritual quest that has led him to find comfort and acceptance in the principles of Buddhism. He walks five miles a day through Waxhaw, calling on shut-ins and others who may need some conversation, or a strong back and a willing pair of hands. He walks through the town cemetery each day to check on and even report current events to our father, our brothers-in-law, and other relatives and friends whose bodies are buried there. Thanks to his own indomitable will and to the daily discipline of his walks, his workouts, and a careful diet, he has grown stronger physically.

But Bill still has no short-term memory. He says daily events flit through his mind and disappear. He can't remember what he ate for breakfast or what he did yesterday or last week. But with that long-term sense of humor, he reports that it is very peaceful not to be able to remember. "Memory can just stir you up," Bill says. "It's restful not to have to worry about yesterday. Gives you more time to enjoy today and tomorrow. I never did live much in my memories, so I don't miss them. I just live in real time."

My brother has learned the art of letting go. To move yourself forward in the water, you have to push the water backward. Some memories are to be savored and kept for a lifetime. Some are to be scuttled. You cannot possibly hang on to them all, even if your short-term memory is intact. Sandburg wrote, "The past is a bucket of ashes." I thought of ashes as weightless and ephemeral until I read Sandburg's account of his daily boyhood chore—disposing of the ashes from the fireplace and the furnace. Curious, I loaded the ashes from our fireplace into a bucket and picked it up. To my surprise, the ashes of the fire, compressed into the bucket, made a heavy load. Then I understood Sandburg's metaphor. The past is heavy to carry. It can be a burden—often a needless one—to hang on to hard memories. Like deleting the deadwood on the computer hard drive, I know I have to delete the deadwood of the past. Lose it. Let it go. Avoid the ever growing weight of the bygone.

Swimming has taught me that I can choose to go forward with life. Propulsion is forward motion after all, and to move onward, I can pull or push on the water as vigorously or as gently as I choose. But if I am to move forward, I have to move the water backward. Then I can live in real time and propel my way toward the future.

SWIMMING PRACTICE

Swimming Lesson Three:
Propulsion

1. Imagine that you have an empty pail to be filled with the ashes from the fireplace. Imagine that the fuel you will burn in the fireplace is deadwood—memories, issues, regrets, grudges that you have been holding onto, but that you need to shed.

—Make a list of all the deadwood you need to burn to ashes.

—Jot down beside each item the reason why you have been holding onto it.

—Imagine yourself tossing it into the fireplace, converting it into ashes, loading the ashes in the waiting pail, and emptying the bucket of ashes.

2. If you are trying to move onward after a difficult experience, write a letter to yourself about it. Divide the letter into three pages, and write as concisely as possible on each page.

—On page one, write to yourself about any lesson you have learned from the experience and any gift the experience has given you. Try not to exceed one paragraph.

—On page two, make a list of the burdens, problems, and/or issues left over from the experience. Cross out the burdens, problems, and/or issues you want to get rid of.

—On page three, make a new list of the gifts and the burdens, problems and/or issues that you want to keep.

—Keep pages one and three. Destroy page two.

—A week from now, read page one again and add any new lessons or gifts that come to mind. Read page three again, crossing out any burdens, problems, and/or issues that you no longer want to keep.

—Repeat this process week by week until page one is full and page three is empty.

3. Write your own Hot Stove Letter—but don't mail it.

4. Review your daily schedule to see if there are any patchwork quilt scraps of time you can use for something you really want to do. If so, write the times and the activity on your calendar. Honor them. Honor yourself by honoring them.

5. Write a letter to yourself using the following prompt: "I need (or want) to propel my way toward the future by _____."

IV. Breathing

When you are swimming, you cannot always breathe when you want to. Sometimes you just have to breathe when you can. Your buoyancy will be impaired if there is not enough air in your lungs. Breathing is more efficient when all the swimming elements are coordinated in a steady and reliable rhythm.

I T IS NOT ONLY in the swimming pool that I can't always breathe when I want to. This is often a daily truth
on the merry-go-round of modern life. Gasping for
breath and for time, we gallop from one obligation to another, working as hard as possible to survive. In too many
places on this planet people live with the daily burden of
hunger and fear, and the daily horror of war. Every human
being—certainly every child—deserves to breathe freely
in a steady and reliable rhythm.

But most of the time, whatever the circumstances, we
just have to breathe when we can. When the lungs are deprived of the air they need, we pay the price of impaired
buoyancy—stress, fatigue, irritability, even estrangement
from the people we love, and from ourselves. Where do
we find the essential time to breathe, to rest, to be? How
do we establish that steady and reliable rhythm?

The first step, I've found, is to simplify, to pare down
to the essence of life. Illness rivets your attention on what
really counts. Twice I have faced the prospect of an illness
that might end my life. The first time, I felt as if I had been
equipped with special glasses that suddenly enabled me

to see in vivid color the facets of life that truly matter. Family. Love. True friends. True work. The life of the mind and the spirit.

I resolved to squeeze the juice and the joy out of each hour. I turned to Thoreau again: "I did not want to live what was not life, living is so dear." The more I swim, the more I try to simplify. To swim cleanly and efficiently, with the utmost power, I need to eliminate wasted motions that result in drag. To live cleanly, efficiently, with the utmost power, I need to discard the unnecessary activity and to banish the wasted motions in my schedule. Otherwise I lose precious time and squander the very breath of my life.

Too many meetings, too many clubs and organizations, too many chores. I had a friend who loved to bowl. She belonged to several bowling leagues and bowled several times a week. For her, bowling was a way to breathe. She often asked me to go with her, but I never did. Even if I had known how to bowl, I needed and wanted to breathe—to use my energy—in other ways. I was working on my first book then and writing was my bowling equivalent. Writing is breathing for me. One day my friend gave up on me. "You poor thing," she said. "You'll never get to bowl." I have no desire to bowl, but she is right that I cannot do all the things I want to do.

Sandburg warned aspiring authors about the renunciations exacted of serious writers. "Deny yourself," he said. Substitute your own aspirations for writing, and Sandburg's axiom is still true. Substitute any other noun—parents, lawyers, teachers, business people, trades people, athletes, musicians, students—and renunciation is part of a disciplined, simplified life. We relinquish one thing for another. We give up the extraneous for the essential. We have to if we are going to be able to breathe.

As I grow older I understand ever more clearly that energy spent one place can't be spent again, and energy squandered is gone for good. I learned this lesson from Grandmother's Dollar. Until Grandmother Ellen died when she was eighty and I was thirty-three, she gave me one crisp, unblemished, brand-new dollar bill for my birthday—a dollar a year for thirty-three years. I was the oldest of her eleven grandchildren, and each of us received a magical birthday dollar as long as Grandmother lived. When I was a child in Waxhaw, this dollar made me feel rich. It seemed to possess unlimited power.

My brother Bill and some of our cousins rushed uptown in Waxhaw to spend the dollar immediately at Niven-Price Company or Miss Texie Austin's dime store. But I tarried with my dollar. I pondered and planned and postponed the moment when I'd have to relinquish the dollar, no matter how much I wanted the treasure it would buy. I knew that if I spent it all for paper dolls, I couldn't buy a bottle of Blue Waltz Perfume. If I turned my dollar over to Miss Texie for a diary with its own lock and key, I couldn't spend it for a book. I loved the power of the decision. As long as I held on to Grandmother's dollar, I kept the power of possibility, the promise of treasures and keepsakes that would give me delight.

I find myself in my sixties spending my energy, my breath, as carefully as I spent those magical dollars. I try to simplify my life so I won't fritter away energy and attention. I want to lavish my energy, my buoyancy, on what really matters.

SIMPLIFYING SOMETIMES means settling for less than perfection. For years I took great pride in keeping house. On the day I turned forty, I suddenly bridled at the prospect of doing the daily household chores that I had imposed on myself. "It's my birthday," I declared to the cats and the dog and the empty house. "I am not going to make the bed or vacuum or do the dishes. I am going to do exactly what I want to." And I did.

That night, Jennifer and her father took me out for a birthday dinner. Then they brought me home. All of a sudden twenty or more friends, who had been hiding upstairs, came trooping down shouting "Surprise!" Thrilled as I was to see them, grateful as I was for the wonderful surprise my husband and child had planned, the first words out of my mouth were, "I didn't even vacuum." I confess that on several birthdays after that, I cleaned the house fastidiously just in case they were planning another surprise party.

Best to relinquish a foolish and futile urge toward perfection than to miss the surprise parties of life. A few years later, seriously engaged in writing, I realized I couldn't write a book the way I wanted to write and simultaneously keep house the way I wanted to keep it. I was going to have to simplify one or the other. When I die, I don't want my epitaph to read: "Here lies Penelope Niven. She died with her floors waxed, her closets organized, and her kitchen cabinets clutter-free." Instead, I want my epitaph to testify that I have been a loving mother, wife, daughter, sister, aunt, and friend; and I have taught, written, and lived with joy. I can't do all that and keep a perfect house.

To breathe is to simplify. People come first. Then writing. Far down near the end of my list you may find cleaning the closets and organizing the kitchen cabinets. But when I do organize the cabinets, run the vacuum, load the dishwasher, shop for the groceries, go to the dry cleaners, wash the car, or do any of those life maintenance tasks, I try to do them with my secondary energy. Swimming has helped me to see that I don't—can't—perform every action with equal energy. I am a morning and afternoon person; my primary energy pours out in the hours between seven A.M. and three P.M. That's when I compose, create, think most clearly, and write most naturally and intensely. With my leftover, secondary energy, I can do the chores, run the errands, keep the accounts, attend to the endless business of writing biography, running a household, helping with the financial and medical affairs of my parents and brother.

Simplifying means putting your best energy to work in your most challenging endeavors. It means choosing where to spend your *self*.

Simplify. Give yourself the guilty pleasure of thirty minutes a day to breathe exactly the way you want to breathe. If you can't spare thirty minutes, give yourself fifteen, or five. (Those "patchwork quilt scraps of time" come in handy here.) Do nothing at all. Do something for sheer fun. In order to breathe during the bleak cold of Indiana winters, my friend Jane Silver and I dressed up appropriately and attended grand openings in our small town—the new microwave-your-own-food cafeteria at one grocery store and the dessert bar at another. When we had to be fitted for bifocals at the same time, we held a bifocal ceremony to commemorate that depressing milestone. We enjoyed a festive annual Secret Pal Gift Exchange Christmas Party, just the two of us, at the Coffee Pot, a restaurant in the nearby countryside. We loved the giant coffee pot on the roof and the sign in the diningroom: "Help Yourself. Children Free at Steam Tables." Since we have wonderful children of our own, we didn't help ourselves to the free children at the Coffee Pot. Fortunately, our families understood that we weren't wasting time in these escapades. We were simply finding ways to breathe.

Make time to have lunch or dinner with a friend, to take a walk in the rain, to write a letter of encouragement or appreciation, to express congratulations or condolences, to savor the sunset, to play with a child, to pet the cat. When we lived on Okinawa, we looked forward to the monthly moon festival. On the night of the full moon, we could hear the music and voices of the Ryukyuan people who gathered on the hillsides, watching the golden moon climb the night sky until its light shimmered far out over the East China Sea. In this monthly ritual, people paused to breathe and to celebrate the turning of the earth, the steady, reliable rhythm of nature.

TO DREAM IS TO BREATHE. A few years ago I realized with alarm that I no longer remembered my night dreams, and I no longer dreamed my daydreams. I had simply stopped dreaming. Dreams are breath to the spirit. I once read about the dangers of interrupted dreams—the dreams buried deep in the heart of hearts—the dreams at the core of us which sustain us or elude us, drive us or frustrate us. I am thinking of the dreams that come to us at night while we sleep, or try to, as well as those that come to us when we are awake because we will them to—the daydreams that reflect our ambitions, our fantasies, our visions of what we could be, of what our lives might be, if only...

Researchers tell us that our dreams have both psychological and biological roots. Dreams mirror the unconscious mind, Freud told us. In these nightscapes, we act out our repressed desires; review problems and experiment with solutions; reveal conflicts to ourselves; continue the lifestyle of the waking hours; seek unity of self by tapping the unconscious sources of knowledge available to dreamers. And if we are deprived of our dreams, we can suffer psychological and even physical damage.

One of my most important waking dreams was to become a mother, and I was elated when my daughter was born. Yet after the first few weeks of sleeping a mother's sleep, always listening, leaping out of slumber at my baby's merest whimper, resting or not resting at the mercy of this new little creature who might or might not sleep through the night, who would or would not wake up at any predictable hour, I began to think about the millions of parents worldwide, through all of time, whose rest and sleep and very dreams were vulnerable to the needs of their children. Interrupted sleep meant interrupted dreams.

Mothers and fathers everywhere have sacrificed their sleep, and thus, their periods of dreaming, for the needs of their small children. It occurred to me that it is a miracle indeed that the world is not overrun by hordes of parents turned into psychological and physical wrecks by the innocent demands of their newborn babies, who have the power from the crib to disturb their parents' sleep and, consequently, their dreams. Whether we are awake or asleep, the dreams we dream are frequently interrupted, postponed, frustrated, and often repressed, forgotten, or abandoned. This is not always the fault of our children—beloved as they are—or our spouses or our bosses or colleagues or society or even ourselves.

Think about the dreams you dream when you are awake rather than the dreams that come to you in your sleep. Actuarial tables indicate that women born in this decade can expect to live to be eighty-one years old. Given the fact that we spend approximately one third of our lives sleeping, the average woman will spend twenty-seven years asleep (if her children and her busy life let her). About twenty of those twenty-seven years of sleep will be spent dreaming, no doubt with interruptions. But what of the fifty-four years spent awake? What about the daydreams—the life dreams? What about the dreams that have been interrupted? Can we keep them? Retrieve them? Put them back together again? Replace them with other dreams? Make any of them come true?

When she was a little girl, my aunt Frances came down to breakfast one morning to report, "I had the most wonderful dream! I dreamed I went to Florida!" Her younger sister Elinor chimed in, "And I dreamed that I went with you!" You have to dream your own dreams, not vicarious dreams, or tag along dreams. Our family motto is "Where there is life there is hope." During the years when I deprived myself of my own dreams—my dreams of writing—I relinquished hope and diminished the possibilities in my life.

I've got my dreams back now. Dreams shouldn't stop when you hit your forties or sixties or nineties. The dreams we dream are of crucial importance in our lives, basic to who we become and what we make of ourselves. "Nothing happens unless first a dream," Sandburg wrote. "In dreams begins responsibility," said the poet William Butler Yeats. And dreams should be spacious, even boundless. When some dreams do come true, they are often reduced in size and scope and possibility. Therefore, I don't want to set out with little dreams, corralled in low expectations. I dream great big, wide dreams. And I breathe long and deep when I dream.

Jesse Jackson said, "If my mind can conceive it, and my heart can believe it, I know I can achieve it." I operate on that hypothesis as I dream, as I breathe. But I am a practical woman as well as an inveterate dreamer. I understand from long experience that sometimes life is less the stuff of dreams and more the stuff of concrete reality. I know there are times when I just have to cope with reality in order to breathe.

If you cannot always breathe when or how you want, you resort to breathing when and however you can. At times this requires some creative coping. My friend Dudley Shearburn, mother of seven children, writes in her delightful book, *Get a Good Life,* about the creative way she coped with getting seven young children clean and fed at suppertime. Three at a time, she put her children in a bathtub full of bubbles and then she sat down at tub side with a platter of Franco-American Spaghetti, cut up weiners, applesauce, and bread and butter. She fed and bathed her children at the same time. You can't always bathe and feed seven children when you want to. Sometimes you just have to do the best you can. Creative coping is a smart way to breathe.

We can be too hard on ourselves at times like these. We need to recognize our limits. I grew up with a Super Mother who cared for home and hearth, husband and children, while she also taught school, directed the church choirs, looked after her mother, and was active in more circles, clubs, and organizations than we could count. In her last year of life, as her health diminished, Mamma spent most of her time in bed. One day my sisters and brother and I were trying to coax her into getting up so we could take her on a brief excursion out of her room. "No," she sighed regally from her bed, one hand on her brow. "A person can only do so much."

Having lived all our lives with the sometimes daunting specter of our mother's high energy and expectations, we were astonished to hear these words come from her mouth. But she was right. A person *can* only do so much, and it is a mark of wisdom to recognize and honor that. And because we can only do so much, it makes sense to choose with care what we will do. Then we are more likely to have time to do it well—and to breathe.

SO OFTEN IN THE face of death people realize that they have squandered opportunities to breathe. Years ago, when a dear friend's young son died suddenly, I went to be with her, to try to help in some practical way as she faced bearing the unbearable. Even as she wept, her face was alight with memories. "I'm so glad I took time to go fishing with him the other day," she said. "I'm so thankful we went to that baseball game." There were very few "If only's" in her litany that day. She had made time regularly during her son's short life to breathe with him. "After all," she told me before his funeral, "we are only promised this moment. Nobody is promised tomorrow."

To breathe, I need time shared with others, especially with those I love. I also need time for myself. Solitude. I need to savor the familiar, ordinary hours, as well as the extraordinary moments. I need to immerse myself in an activity or action that is vital to me: writing. I need the fundamental, steady, reliable rhythm of my work. I depend on it, heart, mind, and soul. As the caricaturist Al Hirschfeld once said, my work is my play. To breathe, I even need the gift of silliness. Jennifer and I think of it as necessary fluff. As you approach the finish line of any prolonged project, as weariness sets in, as you begin to think you will never finish, fluff can help you travel the last miles. As I neared the end of years of arduous work on a biography of Edward Steichen, I stayed at my computer twelve or fourteen hours at a time. Morning person that I am, I was still laboring into the night. How to breathe before going to sleep? I needed to rest and unwind so I could sleep well in order to get up and go at it again the next day. Craving something mindless, I turned on the television set and discovered the world of *Baywatch.* I had never heard of *Baywatch,* but I was riveted—and not just because there was swimming. Every night at 11:00, I left the world of Steichen and lost myself in the fluff of a *Baywatch* rerun. *Baywatch* soothed and diverted. *Baywatch* put me to sleep. *Baywatch* gave me a chance to breathe.

My daughter is a writer and I have tried to instill in her my conviction that to write well—to do anything well— you have to be able to breathe. Because our minds are usually brimming to overflow with the serious nonfiction we are writing, we amuse ourselves faithfully with a daily budget of mindless fluff. For half an hour we escape—perhaps watching television makeovers, or reruns of *My Three Sons, The Dick Van Dyke Show, Will and Grace,* or certain made-for-television movies, such as Donna Mills in *The World's Oldest Living Bridesmaid.* We indulge ourselves by shamelessly following such American pop culture phenomena as *The Bachelor, American Idol,* and *The Pet Psychic.* We read mystery, humor, and romance. We make each other laugh.

The past years have brought us face to face with too much illness and death. We have written through loss, grief, uncertainty, trauma. Jennifer finished her second book four days before her father died of cancer. I can look at every chapter of the books I have written and see in the margins the hard times confronting me in *my* life as I wrote those other lives. We breathe so that we can replenish our resources for the next day's work, so we can carry on.

Carl Sandburg wrote about Abraham Lincoln's habit of joking in the midst of disaster. When someone asked Lincoln why he could be so "light-minded" during tragic times, Lincoln replied, "My God, man, don't you see that if I didn't laugh I would have to cry?" Sandburg surmised that perhaps democracy "can best survive where men know the right moments for complete and solemn reverence or the nonsense that nourishes and the laughter that rests and may even heal."

Allow yourself—even for a few moments a day—the nourishing nonsense, the restful healing of laughter. Breathe.

IN LIVING, as in swimming, we can't always breathe when we want to. We just have to breathe when we can. We have to accept certain inevitabilities; we have to accept and even embrace the natural rhythms and stages of life. I did not realize until Jennifer was born what a trauma birth is for the baby. As I held her that first time, I looked down into her beautiful face and gently touched her forehead, bruised from the forceps. Awash in that staggering tidal wave of maternal love, I was bent on protecting, comforting, and consoling this child, forever. All of a sudden, looking into her dark eyes, I knew that my baby was angry. She was furious at whatever forces had propelled her out of the safety of the womb into this frightening new universe.

Birth hurts. Growth hurts. While the outcome offers certain rewards, there is nothing particularly pleasant about going through puberty. As girls we enter the menstrual years convinced that, despite what our mothers have told us, no one else on this planet has ever had to endure this monthly misery in quite the way that we ourselves have. Some aspects of pregnancy and most aspects of giving birth are difficult and painful. Women fret and struggle through menopause. Men and women rail against old age and take herculean measures to stay young.

I made up my mind a long time ago that I would rather be fifty—seventy—eighty—than be dead. I don't understand why people equivocate about their actual age. I don't mind telling anyone I'm sixty-four. If I were going to adjust my age, I wouldn't tell people I am younger than I am. I'd say I'm ten years older, in hopes they'd say, "But you don't *look* seventy-four!" We often confuse youth with vitality. Some people are born with a robust vitality, a buoyancy of spirit that transcends age and circumstance. This vitality has nothing to do with the calendar and everything to do with the spirit.

Men and women dread the prospect of aging and dying. I used to think that it would have been better if we were born old and aged backward, growing younger and younger until life ended in some timeless counterpart of the womb. But that alternative cosmic design would surely have come with its own set of problems. Ultimately there is nothing we can do to escape these passages of life, and very little we can do to change them to suit ourselves. Puberty happens. Menopause happens. Death happens. It is an act of grace to accept these inevitable seasons of life, to embrace their existence and swim through them, breathing as best as we can. Who knows what waits on the distant shore?

SWIMMING PRACTICE

Swimming Lesson Four:
Breathing

1. Considering your daily schedule, divide a sheet of paper into two columns, heading them as follows:

I can breathe when   I can't breathe when

After you have made your list in each column, review each list for activities you have to do, need to do, want to do—and draw a line through any activity you can eliminate.

2. Write a couple of paragraphs to yourself about ways you can simplify your life, noting any duties, activities, and/or obligations that you can strip out of your schedule.

3. Make a list beginning with the words, "The facets of life that truly matter to me are _____"

4. Divide a page into four columns. First, write a list of your interrupted dreams. In the second column, write "Keep" or "Discard" beside each interrupted dream. Next, write down what you *are* doing about the dreams you want to keep. In the final column write down what you *can* do about each dream you want to keep and convert into reality.

5. Write yourself a promissory note beginning, "I am going to dream a brand-new, spacious dream about _____"

V. The Elementary Backstroke

The elementary backstroke carries you forward steadily with strength and speed. The long glide between strokes allows you to rest as you swim. The elementary backstroke not only uses energy efficiently, it actually conserves energy. When in peril in the water, some weary swimmers have actually saved themselves by relying on the basic backstroke when they were too exhausted to swim using any other stroke.

A SWIMMER NEEDS a variety of strokes and positions of course, but if I had to choose a favorite, it would be the elementary backstroke. Too often we rush through our days with eyes focused downward, heads under water, preoccupied with the immediate moment or the moment to come. The breaststroke allows only vistas of the water itself, alternating with the rhythmical glances to one side or the other, and the occasional glimpse of another swimmer. But the backstroke forces the vision upward—skyward, heavenward—and so it sets me free. At the same time, it connects me to vistas beyond myself.

The elementary backstroke is a languid exertion—the luxurious extension of muscles, the stretch and reach of lungs and heart. Even land-bound exercises such as Pilates or yoga do not yield the deep sensual release of the backstroke. If I consolidate my energy into the power and pull of the stroke, I generate enough momentum to rest and glide. I can propel my way through the expected duties of the day and glide through the unexpected—or glide through the expected and propel through the unexpected, as events demand.

This graceful, seemingly lazy motion is designed to be a shield and source of energy. The elementary backstroke can be beautiful as well as redemptive in its economy. The streamlined stretch and pull, the whip action of the kick, and the grace of the glide allow you to pace yourself and conserve your energy so that you can invest it where it really counts. During the glide, you can give yourself up to the momentum you've generated and just float. You can breathe during the long, easy glissando.

This user-friendly stroke demands that you pace yourself. Conserve your energy—invest it where it really counts. Thanks to the power of the efficient stroke and kick, you can give yourself up to the momentum it generates. You can let each long, deep stroke and kick take you as far as possible, and then enjoy the bonus of the glide. Like the glide of the swan, all motion is below the surface. There should be no splashing, no show, no wasted movement— just steady, reliable progress toward the goal. Sometimes the objective is sheer survival in the undertow of exhausting, overwhelming, even catastrophic events. Sometimes the goal is simply withstanding the normal rigors of daily routine. Always the goal is to move forward.

The elementary backstroke can indeed protect a swimmer from danger, including the depletion of energy or soul stamina. This stroke is very much like putting one foot in front of another when you are land-bound. When you are too exhausted to meet a deadline, complete a journey, fulfill a responsibility, this is the stroke for you.

My swimming lessons have been tried and tested and

have helped me survive. I believed in them before, but they have served me especially well in the crucible of this last year. Yesterday was one of those stroke and glide days when I was beset with detours: A business matter that will require diplomacy and fortitude to unravel. Some thorny problems to sort out with a writing project. Hard decisions to make in a family matter. A hundred e-mails, most of them wanting something, and wanting it now. A snow, sleet, and ice storm that paralyzed the town. A leaky roof. A looming deadline. Profound weariness comes not so much from positive action, forward motion, as from the drag—the downward pull exerted by acts of nature, by circumstance, or by human beings—the inattention, carelessness, neglect, or just plain orneriness of some people.

Just as detours can yield distraction and fatigue, energy can beget energy: I can write all day and into the night, and wake up eager to get my hands on the keyboard again. I love writing, love teaching. When my sisters and I were thinking about going off to college, our parents encouraged us to concentrate on what we loved most, but to get a teacher's certificate in case, they said, you ever have to work. Not in case you have a passion for your work and want to do it with all your might. But in case you ever *have* to work, which when translated meant in case you ever found yourself without a husband or with a husband who couldn't support you properly. I am blessed to have found the work I love and crave to do— perhaps the work I was born to do, no matter what.

I come from a family of intense people. We tend to

fixate on things, even to obsess about them. Whether it is writing music, flying a plane, teaching a class, surveying land, doing cross-stitch, writing a book, running a business, tending the sick, or directing a choir, we are going to do it with total enthusiasm, complete dedication, and utter concentration. We can be downright frightening in our intensity. Early in my work on the Carl Sandburg biography, Jennifer's teacher asked her students on the first day of school to stand up, introduce themselves, and tell about their parents. "My father works at the college," Jennifer said when her turn came; "And my mother is obsessed with this dead guy."

Because I have great energy and a propensity for fixation—I think of it as positive, creative obsession—I have had to teach myself not to do everything with equal intensity. It is self-defeating to glide with the same intensity I invest in the stroke, pull, and kick.

The long journey of writing a biography is like swimming the elementary backstroke. Stroke by stroke, the work carries you forward steadily with strength and speed. The long glide between strokes allows you to rest and reflect as you work, to absorb all you are learning from your journey into another life. When in peril in biographical waters, I can rely on the elementary backstroke when I am too weary to sprint or race.

As I swim in my work, I discover my fellow swimmers, my subjects—Sandburg, James Earl Jones, Steichen, Thornton Wilder—and I discover myself. Each of my books has given me a deeply personal gift—a beacon, if you will—to help me through the journey of my own life. Barney Crile, Sandburg's son-in-law, enabled me to keep on swimming when he taught me not ever to be limited by just what I see on the horizon. He and Helga, his wife, also showed me the joyful imperative of living every day with zest and gratitude.

During my work on the Steichen book, my sisters and brother and I faced the tough decisions so many families wrestle with about how best to ensure the well-being of their elderly parents as they grow older. In their final years, Steichen and Sandburg suffered from senile dementia—and their great shadows hovered in my mind as I watched my own father's brilliant mind ebb and flow and begin to erode. Steichen's granddaughter Francesca Calderone-Steichen, daughter of the physician Mary Calderone, is an authority on elder care, and applied her skills to securing the best health care for her mother. Francesca also guided my family as we sought to secure the best care for our parents, to serve as their informed advocates, and to support them and each other during the diminuendo of their lives.

From James Earl Jones, my daughter and I have learned wonderful practical lessons in how to stay grounded in what really matters in your private life when your public life exerts more and more demands. As my writing partner, James Earl, a stutterer, has taught me that every single word put to the page matters deeply and merits precision of sound and meaning. Words can be sacred. A writer strives to be immaculate with the use of the language.

Interspersed with the pull, stroke, and kick of writing bi-ography, I depend on the long glide and the recovery. I have to live my own life-in-progress at the same time that I am trying to write that other life. When I have been discouraged because of the detours that have kept me from writing a biography of Thornton Wilder, I have said on occasion, "Thornton, you've been dead since 1975. You will have to wait a few months longer." Sometimes we just have to glide, to remember that the elementary backstroke carries us for-ward steadily with strength, if not with great speed.

It took me a while to learn how to stroke and glide when I was out of the swimming pool, but I know now that you need to bear down on the most challenging, creative, significant work with your best energy of the day. Then you can do the least demanding work while you glide. I have learned to write when my energy flows and soars—from early morning until mid-afternoon—and to glide through the chores, errands, dishes, laundry, bookkeeping, and fil-ing in the afternoon and evening hours, when my energy ebbs. A few businesses have experimented with schedules that allow workers to take advantage of their body rhythms, and I wonder how much more productive and fulfilled people would be if that were universally possible.

I have discovered the virtue and value of power naps; even if I don't fall completely asleep, I can usually recharge my batteries in twenty minutes with eyes closed, no music, no distractions. That twenty-minute glide pays off, and I am ready for the next stroke and kick.

When life is hectic, it helps to be able to multitask, as

the efficiency experts say. Parents are especially adept at multitasking. Sometimes we have to do the most important things on the glide and recovery, between the stroke and kick of work and other demands. The glide and recovery yield time to spend with our children, our mates, and our other loved ones, including our friends. The glide and recovery offer time for hobbies, avocations, downtime, rest. The glide and recovery give me space to breathe and to reclaim my buoyancy.

SWIMMING THROUGH exhaustion or peril requires character and courage. "Character is destiny," said the pre-Socratic philosopher Heraclitus. Anyone can swim under optimal conditions. But to swim on despite weariness, despair, or danger is to reach into the depths of your character for resources you may not have known you possessed. This requires courage, and courage does not mean the absence of fear. Courage keeps you swimming despite fear. Courage, derived from the French *coeur*—heart, means you have the heart to keep going despite the anxiety and the struggle. It takes character and courage to summon the strength and willpower to swim through, past, and in spite of obstacles.

You find proof of character and courage within yourself and in swimmers all around you. A single parent makes a strong, solid, loving home for three children. A woman rises to the challenge of rehabilitation and the ongoing recovery from alcohol addiction. A man rebuilds his life after a debilitating stroke. A teacher reaches deep into the lives of her students and, teaching them, reaches far into the future. A nurse and teacher devotes herself to strangers in the backwater of a Southern state and turns them into friends. An elderly man whose senile dementia has cheated him of his powers of speech turns to music instead, creating songs for his family and his caregivers, singing the words with clarity and eloquence, making his listeners laugh and weep. Thousands of strangers pitch in to rescue thousands of other strangers in the wake of an ice storm, a hurricane, or a terrorist attack.

My daughter is one of the most courageous people I know. Stroke by stroke, she has had to swim her way through her parents' divorce; the deaths of her father, three grandparents and other people she has loved dearly; the suicide of a close friend, and the immediate horror of discovering his body; earthquakes, riots, and a stalker during her years in Los Angeles; and the daily grind of earning her living while working to sustain her dreams of writing. She wrote much of her first book at night and on weekends after ten-hour days working at her bread-and-butter job. She wrote much of her second book as her father was dying, pouring out the words in hopes he could read them all, commuting between Washington, D.C., and Minneapolis to spend time with him and share the latest chapter, the latest photographs.

One of the great blessings of being an artist with words, music, or visual images is that you can transmute pain into art. Jennifer's book, like Jennifer herself, is deeper, richer, and wiser because of all she has had to live. She has converted the struggles and the suffering into insight, perception, beauty, grace—art. Stroke and glide by stroke and glide, she has survived the perils of the water. More than that, she has transcended them.

THIS HAS CLEARLY BEEN the year to do the elementary backstroke. Its rhythm lets me alternate motion and rest. Between challenges, I welcome the gentle reprieve of the glide. *When in peril in the water, some weary swimmers have actually saved themselves by relying on the basic backstroke when they were too exhausted to swim using any other stroke.*

If there is a disadvantage to the backstroke it is that you can't see where you are going. You can only see where you've been. When wars loom on the horizon, we often can't see where we are going because we fail to understand where we have been. We can't see the future, and because we don't look carefully enough into the mirror of history, we don't clearly comprehend the past.

In other ways the limited vision of the elementary backstroke can be good practice for life outside the swimming pool. Often we swim blindly, and pay a dear price for such failure of vision. Sometimes we swim by faith, trusting a destination we can't see, but believing that steady progress will get us there anyway. Those elementary strokes often result in changes in our society. In the small Southern town where I grew up, steady strokes— though far too slow and small—finally helped us get rid of some real as well as symbolic plywood walls.

When I was a teenager in Waxhaw, I worked after school and on Saturdays for our town's one and only doctor, who was white. When my father was a boy in Waxhaw there were two doctors—one white, one black—and each of them treated anybody who needed a doctor. One afternoon when he was ten or so, my father rode up town on his bicycle, performed some daredevil maneuvers, and fell off the bike and broke his leg. The white doctor had gone to Monroe, twelve miles away, so it was the black doctor who set my father's leg. In my day, our only doctor was this gentle, honorable, white man who was oblivious to skin color. But in the 1950s, the shameful protocol of segregation dictated that he maintain two separate waiting rooms for his patients, one for white people and one for people of color. He complied by erecting a plywood wall in the middle of the large front room of what used to be a store. There were already two outside entrances, and patients walked through their separate doors into rooms of equal size, identically furnished down to the last chair cushion, plant, and magazine. There was no segregation of treatment rooms, and our doctor treated all citizens of Waxhaw, white, black, and Native American, with equal skill and compassion.

The plywood wall stopped in the dead center of the receptionist's desk so she could serve all the people in those two identical waiting rooms. By the time I was in college, the plywood wall came down at last, thanks to those slow but steady strokes forward, and everybody shared the same waiting room.

When I was growing up, Pearl Vincent, an African American, kept house for us and looked after my sisters and brother and me when our parents were at work. Pearl walked to work and, despite my parents' insistence that she use the front door, entered the house by the back door. She also declined to sit down for meals with us children, but that may have had to do with our table manners and the commotion we made. When she retired, her daughter-in-law, Lou Vincent, took Pearl's place. Lou drove to work, parked her car in front of the house, entered the front door, often sat down for meals with us, and never refrained from chastising us for our table manners.

In 1957, when I was named valedictorian of the Waxhaw High School senior class of thirteen students, Lou listened to me practice my speech, criticized it, and listened to it again until she and I were satisfied with it. By the early 1960s—at last—most segregated schools in the South were gone. In 1968, my sister Doris was salutatorian at the consolidated, integrated high school near Waxhaw. The valedictorian? Gwen Vincent, granddaughter of Pearl, daughter of Lou.

I like to think that the elementary backstroke got us to that momentous evening, steady and sure, eyes on where we had been, moving surely toward where we had to go—where we needed to be.

MY FAMILY AND I have just lived through one of those years when you can't see where you are going. Sometimes I envision a cosmic mother cat who picks us up by the nape of our necks, shakes us gently or forcefully, depending on the occasion, and carries us off to some new place. We don't know where and we don't know why. We just have to believe that the cosmic mother cat has the best interest of her helpless kittens at heart. This has been a busy year for the cosmic mother cat.

How do you keep on swimming through troubled times? You can rely on the basic backstroke to carry you forward steadily when you are too overwhelmed or exhausted to swim using any other stroke. "How are you?" people ask—strangers who wait on you in stores, friends who care about you. "Doing fine," you answer. "Holding up well, all things considered."

This has been a year of peril in the water for almost everyone I know or read about. Yet we have to sustain forward motion. I have relied on the elementary backstroke for whatever progress I have made these past months. People depend on me. I have to earn a living. At age sixty-four, I am keenly conscious of the ebbing of time. I will never write all the books I dream of writing. I will never see all the faraway places I dream of seeing. I will not get to read all the books my daughter will write, teach all the young writers I'd love to teach, spend time with all the friends I want to see, write all the letters I long to write, read all the books, take all the walks, hear all the music, or relish all the adventures I yearn to enjoy. I have to conserve energy here so that I can expend energy there. More than ever, I want to pour my energy into the life that truly matters.

The novelist George Eliot wrote, "It is never too late to be what you might have been." It is clearly too late for me to be an Olympic medalist or a world class ballerina or a concert violinist or another Ginger Rogers. But it was not too late for me to sign my first book contract when I was 44, or my sixth book contract when I was 62. It took a lot of stroking and gliding to reach the day when I got to put pen to paper. But I have discovered that you can go wherever it is you want to go, stroke by stroke, glide by glide, even when you can't see clearly where you are headed or just how you are going to get there.

SWIMMING PRACTICE

Swimming Lesson Five:
The Elementary Backstroke

1. Do you have a positive, creative obsession? If so, write a synopsis of the who, what, when, where, and why of it. Try to confine yourself to one page, single-spaced. If you don't have a positive, creative obsession, write about why you don't. (There is no rule, after all, that says you have to have one!)

2. Write to yourself using the following prompt: "I am exhausted because _____."

3. Now write to yourself using the following prompt: "The best kind of rest and recovery for me would be _____." See if you can make a plan to give yourself at least some of that rest and recovery time.

4. George Eliot wrote, "It is never too late to be what you might have been." Write a Hot Stove Letter (see page 52) to someone you care about who has not yet become the person she/he might have been, and who needs to do something about it. Or, if you prefer, write the Hot Stove Letter to yourself about the same concerns.

5. Write a journal reflection or a portrait of someone you know, using the observation by Heraclitus that "Character is destiny." If you take issue with Heraclitus, explore ways that destiny or circumstance forge character.

VI. Treading Water

You must learn how to tread water. Treading water makes it possible for you to stay afloat in deep water for long periods of time. You must build up your endurance. Treading water is a safety skill that can make the difference between life or death.

THE POET JOHN MILTON wrote, "They also serve who only stand and wait." Because he was talking about patience, fortitude, and survival, his words could apply to swimmers who have to tread water. Sometimes the only appropriate response to life is to stand and wait. Treading water can help you bridge the hard times and the good times. It can save your life.

This safety skill involves your whole body but uses relatively little energy. With your head above water and your body vertical, you scull with your hands and pretend you are peddling a bicycle with your feet. To scull, cup your hands at chest level and stretch your arms to your side and then back beyond your shoulders. Bring your arms back together, letting your hands cross over each other as if you were drawing a figure eight in the water. Then stretch your arms to your shoulders again, making a wide arc. Repeat as often as necessary, establishing as relaxed a rhythm as possible. At the same time, pedal your legs up and down, bending your knees up high toward your chest. Treading water won't take you far, but it will keep you safely afloat for a long time.

Treading water requires patience and some improvisational skills. While there is no official water treading freestyle competition, there should be, for sometimes you have to invent your own comfortable technique and rhythm, in and out of the swimming pool. If you are going to tread water for a long time, you'll want to build some variety into the sculling and pedaling. Be careful, however, not to tread water out of fear, timidity, indecision, lethargy, or sheer laziness, hoping somebody will come to the rescue. And don't keep on treading water when what you really need to do is cut loose and swim.

In the relative security of the pool, treading water is a valuable safety skill when your swimming is interrupted. Perhaps another swimmer suddenly gets in your way, breaking your stroke or throwing you off balance. Perhaps you find yourself caught in water over your head. Perhaps you need to hold your own until someone can reach you to help you out of an emergency. If you get in trouble while you are swimming or sailing in an open body of water, treading water can sustain you until you can be rescued. Whether the interruption is large or small, brief or extended, treading water can serve you well. Stay as calm and relaxed as possible. (I acknowledge that it is difficult to find the middle ground between "Oh, my God, I'm going to die!" and "Relax, relax. Stay calm!" It reminds me of the time a well-meaning neighbor called my brother-in-law at his office and said, "Don't get upset, Andre, but your house is on fire.") Keep your head above water but your arms and legs submerged. Breathe deeply. Sweep your arms and hands through the water, drawing a figure eight. Pedal that imaginary bicycle, letting your arms and legs keep the same rhythm.

Treading water can be a useful exercise in times of emergency on land. Sometimes there is nothing to do but wait: for the law school exam results; for the college acceptance decision; for the verdict about who got the job; for the doctor's diagnosis; for the adoption papers to clear; for a child to be born; for a loved one to come home from war.

Treading water is more than marching in place. It is an act of discipline, persistence, and patience. I have watched three generations of children in our family stubbornly learn to skate entirely on their own, refusing to hold an anchoring hand, falling time after time to the pavement, and rising each time, despite bumps and bruises, to put one skate in front of the other. At last they skate on their own to that "Eureka" moment of balance, poise, and momentum. To enhance his technical skills as a photographer, Edward Steichen photographed a white cup and saucer more than a thousand times one summer, varying the light and the backdrop. Pianists do finger exercises, Steichen said, and these photographs were his finger exercises. Such exercises, in any field, require discipline and patience.

There have been times when I have felt as if I were treading water, especially in my work. As a young high school English teacher, I worried that I was marking time. I did not plan to teach in high school. I set my sights on teaching in a college or university. But when my husband

and I were first married, only one of us could go into a doctoral program. The other one needed to provide the bread-and-butter income. In the early 1960s, the choice was automatic. The husband went to law school or medical school or graduate school. The wife worked to earn the necessary income. The expectation was that the husband, advanced degree in hand, would then become the breadwinner.

I taught English in high school for five years before Jennifer was born. It was rigorous, exhausting, but often exhilarating work. I look back now and see that I was not marking time or treading water. I was serving. I believe in retrospect that I was doing some of the most important work of my life. Teaching, like parenting, can be the most significant, meaningful work on earth. Teaching and parenting lead you to savor the Now, and to relish a child's moments of discovery. A friend told me about one of her first grade students who labored over the shapes and sounds of letters, persisting doggedly until that unforgettable breakthrough moment when the letters and sounds clicked into place. Then he clapped his head and shouted, "My God! I can read!"

Because they may never see the ultimate consequences of their efforts, teachers and parents need to treasure those moments one by one. For the teacher and the parent there is no tidy beginning, middle, and end of work. The student, the son, the daughter are perennial works in progress. "We have to handcraft our children," my friend Jane Silver said wisely. I have always wished as well that I could handcraft my students—tailor each lesson, one by one, to each questing mind and spirit. It is more possible to handcraft one daughter or son, or several, than to handcraft thirty students in one classroom.

As a teacher, I have consoled myself many times by evoking the Scarlett O'Hara Principle: When I have felt that I have not reached Susan or Troy or Malika or Ken in the classroom, I've said, "I'll just think about that tomorrow. I will find a way tomorrow. I will do a better job tomorrow." Students, like daughters, can be wonderfully resilient, flexible, forgiving, and forbearing.

Sometimes as teachers and parents we tread water in order to keep ourselves and our charges afloat. Sometimes we tread water for patience, for endurance, for persistence. Sometimes we tread water so we can rest, absorb, reflect. Sometimes we tread water to savor the moment, to live in the Now. My friend Jane is the mother of two remarkable sons, Mark and Peter. As our children were growing up, Jane and I used to trade children for a few hours or a day at a time. She was appalled that I couldn't sew and, therefore, could not teach Jennifer to sew. (Jennifer and I spring from a family of women who not only sew, but who tat and crochet and make magic with needlepoint, cross stitch, and embroidery. We believe we were denied these talents because we were needed to write books instead. At least, we rationalize the matter that way.) Often on a Saturday, Jane and I swapped children so that she could have a surrogate daughter and I could enjoy surrogate sons.

Jane and Jennifer decked themselves out during their beauty blitzes, trying various kinds of makeup. They sewed—even setting out to make identical prairie skirts. Over at my house, I marveled at how much food and liquid two boys could consume, coached Mark for his speech meets, and drove the boys around town to various adventures and activities. The day I had to cut the rear seat belt of my car to release Peter from an inexplicable tangle, I realized that there was serious inequity in the exchange of one daughter for two sons. But I savored every moment—and welcomed my daughter home with new appreciation.

In the snow belt of the Midwest where we then lived, there was the practical and necessary tradition of the Storm Home. Children who lived in the country were assigned Storm Homes with city families, in the event that a snowstorm took folks by surprise in the middle of a school day. On *A Prairie Home Companion*, Garrison Keillor has ruminated nostalgically about his Storm Home. Although Jennifer, Mark, and Peter lived safely in the city and had no need for an actual Storm Home, they grew up knowing they had the occasional, Saturday Storm Home—that other haven with other adults who loved them, and indulged them; taught them to sew and to orate with fresh patience and enthusiasm; and encouraged them to tread water, catch a breath, trust the moment, savor the Now.

PLANT AND HARVEST a field through continuous seasons, and you quickly deplete the soil. After prolonged, uninterrupted cultivation and growth, the richest earth can be exhausted. Just as fields need fallow time, everybody needs an off-season. Writers, athletes, teachers, and people working in countless other professions can become exhausted and depleted without fallow time. Sometimes, in our impatience to be doing, we deny ourselves that crucial fallow time—floating time—breathing time—treading water time.

My great-aunt Geneva Rone—Aunt Genny—grew a lovely spring garden in the side yard of her house in Waxhaw. Year after year the flowers bloomed in pastel waves—arbutus and crocus followed by jonquils and daffodils, then tulips and irises, then roses. We were visiting one chilly March day, talking in the kitchen with its slanted linoleum floor, eating brownies, and drinking Coca-Cola out of small frosted bottles. We were seldom allowed Coca-Cola or other soft drinks at home, so we frequently ran away to Genny's house, two blocks from ours. She also dispensed unlimited love, comfort, and patience—even on this March day, when Doris, age five or so, went out to play alone in the garden.

Much gossip and several brownies later, we heard Doris slam the front door and run down the hall to the warm kitchen. "Guess what?" she said, eyes shining, clearly pleased with herself. "I went to the garden and I bloomed all the flowers."

So she had. She hardly missed a one. Her fingers had pushed and pulled, forcing open the purple crocus, the yellow jonquils, the pink throats of the tulips. The irises' blue faces were raggedly exposed to the cold March sun. Of course most of the flowers did not survive their embryonic blooming. Frost quickly curled and blackened their premature petals. The March wind tattered blossoms and stems. Aunt Genny's garden was a disaster that year. She patiently explained to Doris that you cannot bloom the flowers on command. They have to bloom themselves, in their own time and way—just as bread has to rise before it bakes, babies have to crawl before they walk, and Christmas can't come in July or September. We have to tread water until spring is ready to come.

I've learned that there are many more things than flowers that you can't bloom on command. You can do your level best to meet a writing deadline—and you should—but sometimes you can't bloom a book. It is growing its own shape and substance. There is the factor of readiness in learning. Children can't be forced to master reading or writing on command. Sometimes love grows slowly, to its own calendar; a relationship can't be forced into bloom. Sometimes I feel like I am treading water endlessly when, actually, I am waiting wisely, if not patiently, for the flowers to bloom on their own.

But sometimes treading water is more than waiting for flowers to bloom. Sometimes it is coping, even improvising, in order to survive. When I was in high school, I was forced to become a majorette. I don't remember exactly why. I was certainly not cut out to be a majorette. I was far more interested in other things: writing poetry, playing the piano and organ, serving as accompanist for the glee club, reading, competing in essay and speech competitions, playing basketball, falling in love. But our high school was very small with very big ambitions. Our elders had notions of grandeur. It was decided that we would have a marching band. With barely a hundred students in the whole high school, every able-bodied student, tone-deaf or not, was required to learn to play a musical instrument—except for Sis Baker, Sandra Rogers, Chicken Simpson, and me.

For some reason that escapes me and that Chicken can't remember (I haven't conferred with Sis and Sandra about this), we were the designated high school majorettes. There were younger ones as well—my cousin Anne McLaughlin, Roberta Howie, and Kathy Bangle, the Methodist preacher's daughter.

While our friends wrestled with bass drums or struggled with trombone or clarinet lessons, we designated majorettes were given instruction in learning to twirl our batons. Sis, Chicken, and Sandra caught on right away, as I recall, and so did the younger majorettes. But I simply could not get the hang of it. Those were the unfortunate days of segregated schools, and the nearby high school for African American students was larger than ours and already the home of a terrific marching band. Our dear friends—three beautiful sisters—went to that school. We did everything together except go to school, and we envied them their band, their cheerleading routines, their football team, and their church choir. Some of my most memorable religious experiences growing up occurred in their church, where the music was sumptuous and the sermons rousing, and where men actually cried at funerals.

The teacher who was trying in vain to help me learn to twirl my baton encouraged me to see if one of the beautiful sisters could help me. My friends tried gamely to teach me to twirl, but they soon gave up; even they could not work miracles to help me conquer the baton.

Why couldn't I have been required to play the tuba or the trombone or the snare drum, as my younger sister Lynn was getting to do? Why the baton? Why me? What was I to do? There was no getting out of this assignment. Everybody else was marching in the band, displaying newfound skills on tubas, trumpets, piccolos, and drums. Aunt Genny was spearheading the uniform committee, composed of every lady within a five-mile radius of the school who could sew. There was no money for real, store-bought uniforms that inaugural year of The Band. But because we were the Waxhaw Indians, the decision was made to garb the band in Indian attire. Aunt Genny and her colleagues solved the problem by adorning existing garments with feathers and fringe. Aunt Genny had found a McCall's pattern for majorette uniforms, and she and the ladies were already stitching white corduroy and trimming it with red braid. They found fluffy little white angora caps that, curiously, struck some of the ladies as something Indian maidens might have worn back in the days before the Waxhaw Indians died of smallpox and measles.

My white corduroy uniform was almost ready for me; my white angora cap was bought and paid for. Someone had wangled an invitation for this novice band of ours to march in the Carrousel Parade in nearby Charlotte, home-made uniforms and all. This was a big city, big time parade, with big time bands wearing real uniforms, led by majorettes who could twirl their batons—even toss them skyward, and catch them—and spin and twirl their way down Trade Street in Charlotte before a crowd of thousands.

Chicken, Sis, Sandra, and the junior majorettes were counting on me. The band was counting on me. Aunt Genny was counting on me. All of Waxhaw was counting on me. I could be a coward and stay home. I could be a sorry majorette and make a fool of myself. Or I could cope. Improvise.

This was my first significant lesson in creative coping. I had to find some way to twirl that baton just to survive. Alone in my room after supper one night, I pulled out the dreaded baton. In front of my mirror I experimented. This was long before I learned to swim, learned that sometimes you just have to tread water.

I was headed toward being the valedictorian of my class. I had won the Voice of Democracy essay contest. I played the organ at the Methodist church. Surely I could outsmart this baton. There must be more than one way to twirl it, I thought—more than one way to move it.

Eureka! It came to me that suddenly. Suppose I just shook that baton as fast as I could. I tried it in front of the mirror. It worked like a charm. I spent hours that night shaking that baton, examining the shaking from various angles. If you shook it fast enough, it looked like twirling.

In fact, it looked like amazingly proficient twirling—twirling faster than the speed of sight.

I practically wept with relief. However, I decided to keep this subterfuge completely to myself. I wouldn't tell Sis, Chicken, and Sandra, much less the junior majorettes. I wouldn't even tell Lynn, my best friend as well as my sister. This coping strategy was born, as far as I could see, out of absolute dire necessity so that I wouldn't let down everyone I knew—not to mention the thousands of strangers lining the streets in Charlotte to watch the Carrousel Parade.

The next time the band practiced, students and faculty alike were stunned by my improvement. "We knew you could do it," they said. Heartened by my success (albeit somewhat conscience stricken by my deceit), I decided to compensate. Now that I was relieved of my failure to twirl the baton, what if I could learn to toss it in the air, catch it, spin, and resume my fake twirling? Not only would that be pretty flashy, it would compensate, I hoped, for my deception.

I practiced diligently and quickly mastered the art of tossing my baton into the air and catching it. Then I reverted adroitly to that vigorous shaking. I was soon awarded the lead position in our lineup of majorettes for the parade. We were awesome in that parade, every single one of us. The band uniforms were a big hit, and by my senior year there were real, store-bought uniforms for the musicians. We majorettes stayed with our white corduroy and red trim. I shook that baton for two years and, as far as I can tell, nobody discerned the difference between my shaking and authentic twirling. I did not confess my deed until just a few years ago.

Because of that baton, I learned the equivalent of treading water. I certainly built up my endurance over the years. Now and then I have a twinge of carpal tunnel pain in my wrists. I get sympathy because I am a writer. Secretly, I think I do not deserve sympathy. This is penance for shaking that baton.

PATIENCE CAN BE a virtue, but it also pays to cultivate the virtue of creative impatience. Sometimes your life depends on treading water, but sometimes it depends on swimming with all your might. The trick is to know the difference. Reeling from the surgeon's recommendation after my breast biopsy, my first response was to acquiesce—to tread water. Then I picked up the phone and called my graduate school roommate, who is a breast cancer survivor. She listened to me for a while, and then interrupted, her wonderful Georgia accent drenching an expletive in diphthongs.

"Shee-ut!" she exclaimed. Creative impatience was encapsulated in that one word, uttered with those reassuring syllables. We could do better than that. We wouldn't wait around. We would find alternatives. And we did.

Creative impatience takes matters into its own hands. Creative impatience says, "No treading water for me. I am going to find a way under, over, around, or through this. I am not going to be daunted by the rough water, the closed door, the brick wall, the high hurdle. I am not going to tell myself *no* or listen to anyone else who is telling me *no*. I am going to tell myself *yes*. I will find a way. I will see this through. I will swim."

Late in her life, the author, playwright, and diplomat Clare Boothe Luce was asked what she considered her greatest accomplishment. She thought a few moments and then replied, "I have survived."

To survive a full life, scathed or unscathed, is a great accomplishment. The swimmer survives sometimes by swimming, sometimes by floating, and sometimes by treading water. Treading water is repetitive, unexciting, even boring—but it is a fundamental survival skill. Knowing how and when to tread water can make the difference between safety and harm, fulfillment and discontent, success and failure, joy and sorrow—life and death.

SWIMMING PRACTICE

Swimming Lesson Six:
Treading Water

1. Are you treading water in any areas of your life right now? If so, list and review them to determine if you are treading water for the right reason(s). Circle any circumstance that has you treading water out of fear, timidity, indecision, lethargy, or laziness—or because you are waiting to be rescued. Think about how you can cut loose and swim.

2. Are you facing a decision that is tough to make? If so, try the age-old strategy of listing the positives and negatives. Or write about it, using the three prompts that debaters use: necessity, desirability, feasibility. (I need it, I want it, I can do it. I don't need it, I don't want it, I can't do it.)

    A. "It is necessary (or not necessary) to do this because _____."

    B. "It is desirable (or not desirable) to do this because _____."

    C. "It is feasible (or not feasible) to do this because _____."

3. If you are in the process of making a decision, write a letter to yourself giving yourself the advice you would give another person in similar circumstances.

4. Did you ever bloom the flowers? Write about when, where, how, and why. Evaluate the outcome of blooming those flowers.

5. List instances of creative impatience that have paid off in your own life or in the life of someone you know. List figures in history or in contemporary life whose instances of creative impatience have paid off for society.

VII. The Breaststroke

With this stroke, you breathe in rhythm with the pull, and your face is submerged during the glide. You can easily convert the breaststroke to a semi-vertical position which allows you to hold your head up. This way, you can see your fellow swimmers and communicate with them if you wish.

THE BREASTSTROKE has been called the oldest swimming stroke, as well as the most popular one. Although this graceful, reliable stroke has long given pleasure to recreational swimmers, it is considered the slowest racing stroke. Advanced swimmers, however, can endow it with surprising power and speed. Like the elementary backstroke, the breaststroke rhythm includes a glide and, for many swimmers, a whip kick rather than the more traditional frog kick. Unlike the elementary backstroke, the breaststroke allows you to see where you are going, and to see your fellow swimmers and communicate with them if you wish. This is especially true if you choose to adapt the stroke to a semi-vertical position and hold your head up.

Unless you are part of a water sports team or a water ballet troop, swimming is a solitary sport. You can't swim well in water polo or water ballet if you can't swim well solo. Even when you are a part of the camaraderie of a swim team, much of your practice and performance time is solitary. In swimming, as in relationships, you really can't do *together* until you learn how to do *alone.* When you are truly comfortable swimming alone, being alone, and living alone, you are more likely to swim, be, and live comfortably in intimacy with others. Love, someone said, is intimate communion.

Once my father and I were driving through the North Carolina countryside on the way to join our family at the beach. We talked for an hour or two about many of the topics that interested us—religion, politics, Carolina basketball, our favorite writers, crazy things that people do. Then we rode for nearly an hour without words. After a while, Daddy said, "It's not easy to be quiet with most people. Thank you for that companionable silence." My father also liked to quote Proverbs 17:28: "Even a fool, when he holdeth his peace, is counted wise." In one of the books in his library, he had underlined a sentence from Benedict de Spinoza's *Ethics:* "The world would be happier if men had the same capacity to be silent that they have to speak."

Perhaps it is because the women in our immediate family and our family at large far outnumber the men that my father deeply appreciated a meaningful silence and preferred it to meaningless chatter or purposeless speech. Not that the women in our family are prone to purposeless speech. Meaningless chatter sometimes, but even then there is a purpose. I've always appreciated the companionable silence I spend with my own thoughts. Even more, I treasure the companionable silence I shared with my father, and can share with a few others.

Swimmers often experience the companionable silence of stroke, pull, and glide in water they navigate with fellow swimmers. More often, in and out of the swimming pool, we try to communicate with sound rather than silence. Psychiatrists and marriage counselors have done some useful work on family systems of communication that could help us in global communication on the world stage. Some families fail to communicate clearly because they seem to speak with their faces submerged, as if they were swimming under the water during the glide in the breaststroke. They don't look each other in the eyes. They don't listen to each other. Underwater, they can't hear or speak clearly. They need to adapt—to hold their heads above water so they can see, hear, and speak to each other clearly.

Southerners often find direct communication especially difficult. At her mother's knee, a Southern woman of a certain age learns tact and guilt. She learns almost by osmosis to be tactful about any situation, and feel guilty for any sin, whether or not she has committed it herself. Tact is, at root, a genteel form of diplomacy. I think tact in the Southern woman is a lingering legacy of the Civil War. I can imagine a Southern lady saying, on first encounter, "I wonder, General Sherman, if it wouldn't be better for everyone concerned if you and your men refrained from burning down my home?" However, lest General Sherman or anyone else failed to see the strength in her tactful gentility, the Southern lady knew how to take her stand. Where home and hearth were concerned, she could quickly be pushed way past tact to a formidable resolve.

You have heard of the steel magnolia—a tradition far more than a cliché.

I resolved as a young mother to teach my daughter to communicate as directly and forthrightly as possible. This goal grew out of the years I had already spent trying to navigate the hazardous, roundabout, often inscrutable avenues of tactful and indirect conversations. It was also due in part to the fact that I was a married woman with a child and my mother had never yet spoken the word "sex" in my presence. I was sixty and she was eighty-three when that word first fell from her lips to my ears, and I was stunned to hear her say it, albeit relieved to know that the word existed in her vocabulary. To further complicate matters, I had married a taciturn man who expected me to regularly and reliably read his thoughts. Southern women are remarkably skillful at mind reading, but I was growing tired of it.

Southern heritage aside, I set out early on to guide my daughter in the ways of direct communication. "Words matter. In fact, words can be sacred. Say what you mean. Mean what you say." Still there is a delicate balance between tact, good manners, and candor. At dinner one night, Jennifer, age four, pronounced the tuna casserole yucky. "Don't call it yucky, dear," I chastised. "If you don't care for something, just say so politely."

Soon afterward, we were having dinner with friends. Spinach was being served. Jennifer hated spinach even more than tuna casserole. Before I could give her a "Please don't say yucky" look, the bowl of spinach reached Jennifer's hands.

"No thank you," she said sweetly. "I don't care for any. But if I liked spinach, I know I would really enjoy it."

She was only four and she had already mastered the skill of consummate tact. Fortunately, she has grown into an independent-minded young woman who can, most of the time, say exactly what she means and mean what she says. Like her mother, she is sometimes beset with reluctance when it is necessary to say tough, frank words, contentious words. The Tact Reflex sometimes gets in the way. But we are writers. Words matter to us. "In the beginning was the Word...." Writers live in words, live by words.

Words can confuse and harm, anger and agitate. But sometimes the most important words are the words that go unsaid. I recently ordered a gift for Jennifer by telephone. When I was asked what to say on the card, I replied, "I love you more than words—Mom."

"That's nice," the voice on the phone said. "My mother has never in my life told me she loves me."

Why? I wondered. How could a parent withhold those words? How can words of love, praise, encouragement, and appreciation be held back? How to measure the harm to the person who deserves to hear those words, and to the person who declines to speak them? How many world problems have at their root a failure to communicate? There are about one hundred official languages on this earth, and countless dialects and tribal or regional variants of languages. There are words in all of them to express a universal human impulse: See me. Hear me. Know me as I am.

THE BREASTSTROKE is a particularly appropriate stroke for a swimmer who writes. I knew when I was five that I would be a writer, and my parents were steadfast in support of my imagination. They never expected me to color within the lines. They read to me, talked to me, and listened to me as if I had important things to say.

Waxhaw was a microcosm for the wider world, and a useful laboratory for a writer. I learned to *listen* at a very young age—on the front porch of our house, my great-grandmother's house, and Aunt Genny's house, and on Grandma and Grandpa Gamble's side porch over on Providence Street. (The Gambles weren't really my grandparents, but in our extended family, I believed they were. They welcomed us to their porch, but Grandpa Gamble was not shy about sending people on their way soon after dark. Regular as clockwork, he'd rise from his rocking chair and say, "Come on, Grandma. Let's go to bed so these folks can go home.")

Early on in Waxhaw, I learned people's histories and characteristics, their flaws and strong points, and a good many of their secrets—and they knew mine. I heard oral history long before I knew the term. I discovered my own family history, including some mysteries, in the letters, scrapbooks, and newspaper clippings stored in the window seat upstairs in my grandmother's house. I began to read biography voraciously. Decades before I imagined writing biography, I was learning some of the tools of the trade.

Like the swimmer doing the breaststroke, the biographer works for prolonged periods with her head submerged during the glide, then holds her head up so she can see and hear. I believe that the biographer should be unobtrusive—an invisible man or woman, submerged in the water. The reader should see only the subject's life, not the splashing or kicking of the biographer. That is difficult, if not impossible, as hard as some of us do try to stay out of the reader's way. A biography is also inevitably and subliminally about the biographer's life. You spill your own life onto the page no matter how hard you try to stay invisible in the shadows. Your soul gets written into your work, someone warned Sandburg. This is true of any person doing any work.

Biography is essentially a meditation on life, an exploration of the mystery and meaning of the human condition. Whose life is this anyway? I sometimes wonder as I work on a biography. I have to be careful not to confuse reliving and writing those other lives with *becoming* those other people. Toward the end of two decades of work on his biography of Abraham Lincoln, Carl Sandburg began to act and dress and look like Lincoln. I made my family and friends promise to warn me if I started to look like Carl Sandburg.

"Where to? What next?" he wrote in a poem. With the breaststroke, you can see where you are going, although there is no guarantee that you'll be able to see what comes next. That is one of the reasons I love writing biography. At least I know how that other life is going to turn out.

THE BREASTSTROKE allows you the selective solitude of swimming true to form, head submerged, then lifted to breathe, then bowed again in that near-silent world under water. This traditional stroke allows you privacy, the company of your inward self, while the modified breaststroke lets others into your world. When you hold your head up you can see your fellow swimmers, engage them in conversation, communicate. You can choose to strike a comfortable balance between companionship and solitude. In any life, that balance is the key. Ralph Waldo Emerson advocated such a calibration of companionship with others and companionship with self: "It is easy in the world to live after the world's opinions; it is easy in solitude to live after your own; but the great man is he who in the midst of the crowd keeps with perfect sweetness the independence of solitude."

In our family, there was a Niven uncle, several generations back, who was a hermit. We don't know why he chose to be a hermit or where he sequestered himself, for how long, or to what end. Perhaps this mysterious uncle simply agreed with Thoreau, who wrote in *Walden*, "I never found the companion that was so companionable as solitude." There is something of the hermit in all of us—the need for time alone; time away from others; time to settle down into ourselves and simply be who we are without masks or defenses.

My great-aunt Sallie Marsh Griffin was called eccentric, even crazy, by people of little imagination, including certain members of her own family. A widow and childless, Aunt Sallie never conformed to what her family saw as her predestined role as a quiet, demure, retiring widow. She traveled, she read, she argued, she wrote, she even sent herself away to college in Chicago, Illinois, far from Marshville, North Carolina, where she had lived all of her life. She corresponded with people she knew and with people and institutions who, in her opinion, simply needed a word of cheer and encouragement. After she died, I saw among her papers a note of acknowledgment: "Dear Mrs. Griffin: We at the Mount Olive Pickle Company always enjoy your Christmas card, and we thank you for the one you have sent to us this year." When Aunt Sallie went to live in a nursing home, she enlivened her days and the days of the staff with mischief and whimsy. On one visit, I was told by a concerned nurse that Aunt Sallie insisted she was going ice skating. There was no ice. Aunt Sallie had no ice skates.

"What's this I hear about ice skating, Aunt Sallie?" I asked.

She answered with the customary sparkle in her vivid blue eyes: "Oh, I know I can't go ice skating, and you know I can't go ice skating—but it gives the nurses something to think about besides sick old people." She told me more than once, "I have to spend so much time with myself. I want to be good company." We should all prize ourselves as much as Aunt Sallie did and make sure we are good company for ourselves. If we let ourselves down that way, we'll almost certainly fail to be good company for other people.

A friend wrote in a poem, "Bring only who you are." It is a rare friendship that allows you always to bring only who you are. Solitude is essential for the ongoing discovery of who you are, and companionship is necessary for the fullest expression of who you are. And always, you live in your own company. As Ram Dass says and Clint Black sings: "Wherever you go, there you are."

Sandburg spoke often of creative solitude and the necessity for an artist to be alone with his work. He told Ezra Pound, "You have to learn to eat loneliness and like it." This creative, chosen solitude is different from the loneliness of isolation. Theologian Paul Tillich wrote, "Language has created the word *loneliness* to express the pain of being alone, and the word *solitude* to express the glory of being alone." Novelist Thomas Wolfe believed loneliness to be "the central and inevitable experience of every man." Tennessee Williams put this line into the mouth of a character in his play *Orpheus Descending*: "We're all of us sentenced to solitary confinement inside our own skins, for life!" It helps to know that others feel that solitary confinement as well.

I am indeed alone in here, inside my own skin. What do I say to myself when I am alone? Am I on speaking terms with myself? Will I be at home with myself if circumstances deprive me of the intimate daily companionship of people I love?

We are not alone in this essential loneliness. We do not have to stay submerged in lonely waters. We can swim with heads up, hands outstretched. We can allow other people into our lives. We have the power of choice. This is not to minimize the challenges of solitude. Many people are terribly afraid to be alone. Sandburg spoke of this in a poem based on a letter he had written to a friend who sought advice for his teenaged son:

Tell him to be alone often and get at himself
and above all tell himself no lies about himself
whatever the white lies and protective fronts
he may use amongst other people.
Tell him solitude is creative if he is strong
and the final decisions are made in silent rooms.

In his cabin at Walden Pond, on the edge of his hometown, Thoreau reclaimed his solitude and staked claim to his soul. He described it this way:

What was the meaning of that South-Sea Exploring Expedition, with all its parade and expense, but an indirect recognition of the fact that there are continents and seas in the moral world to which every man is an isthmus or an inlet, yet unexplored by him, but that it is easier to sail many thousand miles through cold and storm and cannibals, in a government ship, with five hundred men and boys to assist one, than it is to explore the private sea, the Atlantic and Pacific Ocean of one's being alone.

A fundamental part of our purpose on this earth "is to explore the private sea, the Atlantic and Pacific Ocean of one's being alone." This journey into the private sea is vital to the growth of the soul and the evolution of the fullest, truest self. We will pay a high price if we avoid or ignore that essential, rudimentary journey. To forego the exploration of the private sea is to jeopardize the discovery of the truest self.

We don't teach our children to walk. The power to learn to walk is born in them. Unless that power is hindered by some infirmity, the child arrives at the will, drive, and readiness to walk, and works out the logistics for herself, frequently tumbling and falling, but climbing up again to take a few more clumsy, faltering steps. Finally—one step after another—she is walking, then running, then dancing, at home on her own two feet. This metamorphosis is a mirror for the exploration of the inward life. The power, the need, the will to know the self is born in us. We have to work out the logistics of the exploration for ourselves. We will frequently tumble and fall, but if we keep at it, we will eventually find the home within.

We are richly blessed indeed when we feel at home in the oceans within, as well as in the oceans out there where all the others are.

SWIMMING PRACTICE

Swimming Lesson Seven:
The Breaststroke

1. Sometimes the most important words are the words that go unsaid. Make a list of the words you wish you had said, or could say, to someone you love. Say them if you can.

2. Make a list of the words you wish that someone you love had said or would say to you. Then communicate with that person if you can.

3. Write to yourself about solitude, beginning with the prompt, "I love (or hate) to be alone because _____."

4. Write a description, make a photograph, draw a picture, or otherwise identify and illustrate the physical place—the house, the room, the garden or woods or river or other place in nature—where you feel most at home.

Explain why. Do the same for the physical place where you feel least at home.

5. Write about your inner sense of home, beginning with the prompt, "I feel (do not feel) at home within myself be-cause_____." Then continue, using the prompt, "I may learn to feel more at home within myself if I try _____."

VIII. Diving

*It is best to master the proper position and sequence
of the dive before you try it at significant heights.
Once in progress, a dive has to be completed,
for better or worse. It moves at its own gathering
speed and momentum. Never dive into waters of
inadequate depth. Serious injury is almost a certainty
if the water is too shallow.*

WHEN MY BROTHER BILL was a gawky ten-year-old, he was sent off to the mountains for a week at Camp Tekoa, a summer camp run by the Methodist church in the fragrant pine woods near Flat Rock, North Carolina. I was a counselor at the camp that summer, and Bill was mortified to have his big sister lurking about. He made me swear not to tell anyone I was his sister or to interfere in any way with his life and newfound freedom at camp. I promised. When he was assigned to sit at my table at supper one night, we went around the circle introducing ourselves. "I'm Penny Niven from Waxhaw, North Carolina," I said. "I'm Bill Niven from Waxhaw, North Carolina," Bill said when it came his turn. No one asked whether we knew each other, we two Nivens from that very small town. As far as anyone could tell, we were total strangers.

I didn't worry about Bill during the daily swim in the deep, clear lake in the center of the camp. After all, a real swimming instructor had taught him to swim in a real swimming pool. I didn't even worry when I saw him leaping off the low diving board, gangly arms whirling like a windmill. But I wanted to run after him and pull him down to safety when I saw him climb the steps of the high diving board and wait his turn to hurl himself into the cold water below. I knew my brother had no experience diving from such a height. No doubt some macho dare had driven him up those steps, to stand shivering in the sunlight while he waited his turn to plummet into space. I was horrified, but I had promised. I would not intervene and humiliate my brother. Instead, I spoke discreetly to a lifeguard, alerting him that the tall skinny boy with the curly brown hair was a diving novice, about to plunge off the high board with no experience at significant heights, and no knowledge of the proper position or the sequence of the dive. Then I prayed.

Bill's dismount was a leap more than a dive, and he hurtled toward a sure head-on collision with the water. But it was too late to turn back. *Once in progress, a dive has to be completed, for better or worse.* He moved with gathering speed and momentum, hit the water with a resounding splash, and, after what seemed to me a very long time, bobbed up to the surface of the lake grinning, very pleased with himself. He did it, and he survived. By the end of the week, Bill was almost as proficient as his buddies, waiting his turn, cocky in the sunlight, and swaggering when he got out of the water. Bill was too embarrassed, stubborn, and determined to settle. He was willing, despite the danger, to risk stretching and diving from the greatest height into the deepest water.

It can be far more dangerous to settle than to stretch,

more risky by far to dive into water that is too shallow than into water that is too deep. Almost all the regrets of my life are about settling for the shallow end of the pool rather than stretching for the depths. There are private, personal moments as well as professional moments when I settled rather than stretched. Too often we take refuge in the shallow water and live to wonder what might have been. Holding back from challenges and change can stifle the mind and calcify the spirit. Sometimes we choose to dive into the deep water. Other times, however, we are forced off the high dive by life events: an unexpected promotion; a job loss; an economic blow; a death in the family; divorce; illness; accident; war.

It took years of living for me to summon the courage to hazard the deep water in my writing life. First I had to find the courage to fail. As long as I dreamed about writing but found dozens of excuses for not writing, I was safe. What if I tried and failed? What then? Wasn't it better to hold on to the dream than to test it, try it, and fail? It was terribly hard, terribly frightening to pull myself out of the safe, shallow waters and dive into the deep end of the pool where I couldn't even see the bottom. But when I found myself in my forties, astonished at how quickly the decades had passed, I knew I had to jump off the high dive soon or I never would. Like my little brother at that long-ago summer camp, I had to drag myself up the steps, stand there shivering in the sun, and leap off into the unknown.

One of my motives for learning to swim was to grow in flexibility as well as resiliency. Arthritis plagues many people in my family, and it comes to my sisters, brother, and me through both family lines. As I wrestled with the fears and worries that kept me from writing, the first symptoms of arthritis emerged in my fingers. I believe that swimming and writing have been healing therapy, forestalling most of the stiffness and pain of arthritis. So far it only afflicts my hands, especially when I am not writing. I don't yet have to parcel out the key strokes as I did Grandmother's magical dollar. It is when the cosmic mother cat keeps me from writing that my hands become stiff and my fingers hurt. When I am writing—thereby exercising them with the work I love to do—my fingers fly.

It is better to try something and fail than to try nothing and succeed, my friend's sugar packet had told me. I found exhilaration as well as fear in my first high dive, thrill as well as challenge. As I began to grow into myself as a writer, that passion for writing shoved me out of the shallows into new depths in the life of the mind. Every single one of us is born with a gift, a talent—at least one. We are responsible to and for those gifts. They never leave us alone. Unused, they make us restless, unhappy, even bitter. Used to the hilt, they fulfill us, giving us that "vast measure of content" that one poet speaks of in the lyrics of a song. When Jennifer finished graduate school, poet Maya Angelou spoke at the commencement exercises. She admonished the graduates to honor their gifts, to use them, share them, and live up to them. She left the students with a challenge ringing in the summer air: "Get out there and deserve your genius."

To deserve your gift—your genius—you cannot settle for the safe, serene waters in the shallow end of the pool. You have to fling yourself off the high dive, soar briefly skyward, then dive into the depths. Life changes force us into the deep water. Death forces us into deeper waters. Call the roll of losses in your own family. I salute both my stalwart grandmothers and both my sisters, who as widows grew to be at home in and, eventually, through grace and strength, to thrive in the deep waters. My cousin Patsy and her daughters still reel from the shock of the accident that killed husband and father Charles McGee on a balmy April evening, just before dusk. None of us can believe it yet. Jennifer reshapes her life as she copes with her father's illness and death. I feel twice-widowed. I lost him to divorce. I lost him to death. My father is dead. My mother died last spring. This is drama, but this is not a play. There is no dress rehearsal. We have no script. We don't know the lines. We have to make them up as we go. We have to perform them live, on the spot, no chance to go back and start over from the top. What will we do? How will we stand it? The questions haunt us as we bear the unbearable, and lead us, unbidden, often dragging our feet, to new depths—to new chapters of life.

IT NEVER OCCURRED to me until Jennifer's senior year in high school that we do live our lives in chapters—rich, rollicking, mysterious, painful, often unwieldy chapters. When Jennifer was in first grade, her teacher planned Career Week—an ambitious if somewhat irrelevant project for first graders. Nevertheless, all the fathers—this was the 1970s—were invited to come and talk about their work. As the grand climax of Career Week, each child announced his or her career plans. Jennifer had decided by Friday that she would be a teacher. The next morning, she came to the breakfast table weeping. "Oh, Mommy," she sobbed. "I made a big mistake. I promised to be a teacher. Is it too late to change my mind?"

I hugged and soothed at length, trying to convince my child that it certainly was not too late to change her six-year-old mind about her career. "You can be anything you choose," I promised her. "You can decide later." Over the years, Jennifer moved through many chapters of career choices: detective, rock star, archaeologist, rock star, astronaut, Mouseketeer, writer, actress, veterinarian, president of the United States, rock star. I wanted my daughter to dive into the deep water with gusto. Yet it was so much easier to urge her toward the high dive of her aspirations than to imagine such a life for myself.

You grow up and you go to college and you marry and you work. The children come and you are too busy to breathe in your thirties and early forties and all of a sudden you are taking them to college. You cry all the way home, using whatever you can find to absorb your tears. For me, it was the Flintstones towel Jennifer had left in the car. I wept onto Wilma Flintstone's and Betty Rubble's terry cloth shoulders all the way from New Jersey to North Carolina after I deposited my precious only child in her dormitory room at Drew University. I shed so many tears

I could hardly see by the time I drove over that last hill toward home. How did it happen so fast? How could I live without that treasured child under my roof? My life might as well have been over.

Home, I found that someone had left a basket of late summer peaches on my doorstep. They were still warm from the orchard and the dying sun. That lovely, simple gift cheered me. "I wish I could just eat fresh peaches for supper," I sighed. Reflexively, however, my mind ran through the four basic food groups, and I scanned the pantry for ingredients to assemble a healthy, balanced meal. Then it struck me. I had only myself and the cat to feed, and I could eat anything I pleased. I could feast on fresh peaches this night, and the next, and the next— so long as the peaches held out. For the first time in my life, I could eat whatever I chose. I could go on a peaches binge, and no one would ever know—and if they did, it didn't matter. I wept over those scrumptious peaches, surely the most succulent, sensuous, beautiful fruit in paradise. I would cook any kind of feast to have Jennifer home again. But it was time for Jennifer to fly, to dive.

I would find my consolations where I could—in peaches for supper, in this enforced opportunity to discover and rediscover myself. Recently divorced, I had to finish furnishing my new home. I grew up in my parents' home in Waxhaw and lived with furnishings they chose. I went to college and graduate school and lived in furnished dormitory rooms. My first apartment was furnished with hand-me-downs and odds and ends. Jack and I furnished our first little house with more hand-me-downs and odds and ends. Then we began to buy furnishings we chose together. After forty-seven years of life, nearly twenty-three of them spent in marriage, I had no idea on earth what my taste was, what I would choose if left to my own devices. I could hardly wait to find out.

Suddenly I realized that, by circumstance more than choice, it was Penelope Time. Now, for the first time in my life, I was solely and completely responsible for choosing my furniture, planning my menu, living my life, following my dream. It was terrifying. But it was also tempting—tantalizing. And what a marvelous surprise to discover, sans husband, child far off at college, nest empty—and a new nest at that—that there was a new chapter to be lived. And more chapters to come, full of mystery, promise, possibility. I could not have stayed safe in the shallow water if I had wanted to. Fate—destiny— the cosmic mother cat—had forced me to dive into the deep waters. For better or worse. Sink or swim.

Now I see, looking back on my life and looking ahead, that I could easily break my neck—my spirit—if I dive into the shallows. If I were a sailboat I could easily run aground there on the shoals. Contrary to what I believed years ago, more dangers lurk in the shallow waters of certainty than in the deep, deep waters of possibility.

I like to think of myself sometimes as soaring in the midst of a dive from a significant height into waters rippling with promise. Once in progress, the dive has to be completed—for better or worse. I am doing all I know to do, all I can learn to do, to make it be for better. The dive moves at its own gathering speed and momentum. The water is deep, but I am at home there now. I embrace the depths. I am buoyant. I can breathe, propel myself onward, float and glide when I want to, tread water when I have to, swim like crazy when I must.

And when this chapter of my life is finished, I'll just climb out of the water, mount the steps one more time, stand in the sunlight a moment, high above the deep, waiting water—and I will dive.

SWIMMING PRACTICE

Swimming Lesson Eight:
Diving

1. Make a list of situations in your life when you have settled rather than stretched, and reflect on the outcomes.

2. Make a list of the times in your life when you were forced off the high dive by life events: a promotion; the loss of a job; your own illness or the illness of someone close to you; divorce; a death in the family; war. Beside each item on your list, express in a line or two the most valuable outcomes of that forced dive into deep waters.

3. Are you holding back from some opportunity or action because you are afraid to fail? If so, write yourself a Hot Stove Letter giving yourself advice about how to get out of the shallow end of the pool.

4. Make a list of at least five talents or gifts you possess. Don't be modest. Then divide a sheet of paper into four columns. In Column One, list your gifts/talents in order, the greatest gift/talent on top. In Column Two, list them in order of the gift/talent that you use most. In Column Three, list your gifts/talents in order of the sense of fulfillment they give you.

In Column Four, list your gifts/talents in order of the pleasure and fun they give you. Now review the four columns to determine what, if anything, they tell you about how you are exercising your responsibility for those gifts.

5. Write an imaginary Table of Contents for your life, dividing it into chapters, beginning with Childhood. There can be as many chapters as you want there to be. Once you arrive at the current chapter, name the chapters that, according to your plans, hopes, and dreams, lie ahead.

IX. Swimming Alone

One of your highest goals as a swimmer is to feel at home in the water, and to feel at ease with your preparation to handle any water emergency. Try not to swim alone. Try to swim with someone who can help you or get help if there is an emergency. If an emergency occurs when you are swimming alone, rely on all the skills and experience you have developed over a lifetime of swimming. Use your head as well as your body. Trust and respect the power of the water.

THE TIME COMES when I have to swim alone, one way or another. Swimming alone is not a competitive, comparative enterprise. This is not about out-swimming other people. It is about swimming the best swim I can muster, and feeling at home in the water.

Soon after I started swimming alone as a writer and feeling tentatively at home in the biography waters, I heard that another writer was thinking about writing a biography of Carl Sandburg. My first impulse was to get out of the water and clear the way for him. He had far more experience—and a Ph.D. He was older and wiser. He would surely write a better book. I thought I should just climb out of the pool and let him have it all to himself.

At the time I was reading *The Notebooks of Martha Graham,* which my literary agent, Lucy Kroll, had shepherded into publication some years earlier. I came across Martha Graham's observation about what writer Brenda Ueland calls "the Incomparable You." As Graham puts it, "There is a vitality, a life force, an energy, a quickening, that is translated through you into action, and because there is only one of you in all time, this expression is unique. And if you block it, it will never exist through any other medium and will be lost. The world will not have it."

This was an epiphany for me. There is only one of you in all time. Only one of me. Your capacity for expression is unique. So is mine. No matter how many biographers write biographies of Carl Sandburg or any other figure, no one book will be like any other. Each writer's expression is unique. Only I can write the book I am given to write. I can't write anyone else's book. No one else can write mine. And if I block my expression, or you block yours, "it will never exist through any other medium and will be lost. The world will not have it."

It is a sacred responsibility to convert your unique, incomparable life force into positive action—into creative, constructive expression. There is only one of you in all time. Only you can do the work you have been given to do. If you do not do it, the world will not have it. This is not to inflate the importance of the work that you do, that I do, or that any one person does. I have come to see all of us as vital instruments endowed with some sacred trust. We are given breath and energy, minds and hearts, gifts and vision. The world needs the best manifestation of your incomparable self, and mine. If we block the expression of the gifts we have been given, we cheat the world and we cheat ourselves. If we deny, distort, abuse, neglect, or misuse the gifts we are given, we do great harm to others and ourselves. We have no power to determine the gifts we receive, but great power over how we use them. How we invest ourselves. How we swim.

I suppose my sense of vocation comes from Grandmother Ellen. She believed she was meant to work as a
nurse and a teacher. These were not simply jobs. Her vocation, her mission, was to serve. She did it with her
whole being, with integrity. Unity. Wholeness. Complete-
ness. She lived near Cross, South Carolina, on the verge of
the massive swamps of the Santee River. For a time she
sold encyclopedias, filling her little old black coupe with
sample books and bumping along the rutted backroads
that zigged and zagged around the marshes. Grandmother
literally transported knowledge to the backwater cabins
with the fervor of the countless bootleggers who plied the
remote, mysterious creeks feeding the river. I've been told
Grandmother would sell a set of encyclopedias to a family who had no money and couldn't read. Then she would
help them find ways to earn the money and she'd teach
them to read, usually throwing in some free nursing services along the way.

Grandmother felt a deep Presbyterian, predestinarian
duty to serve. She and her children and children-in-law
instilled that fearsome, even sacred sense of mission in
their children. We have chosen many avenues of service,
my ten cousins and I; but we do our work with fervor and
a keen sense of purpose, if not destiny. To us a job is more
than a job. It is a mission. Grandmother said so. Work
deepens the meaning and purpose of life when work is
embraced as vocation, as service.

You don't have to be a missionary to have a mission,
Grandmother said. I grew up in the Methodist church, and

when I was about twelve, answered an altar call at a stirring revival service during a week of services at Pleasant Grove Camp Meeting near Mineral Springs, North Carolina, a few miles from Waxhaw. Actually, I answered several altar calls that week, alone at first, but then leading a growing procession that included my sister Lynn, our cousin Patsy, our dear friend Loffie Nesbit, and several other willing children. As the week wore on, my parents grew concerned about my motivations. At my mother's behest, my father finally took me aside to discuss the matter. I explained that I thought it was my duty because the preacher was preaching so hard, so few people were marching up to the altar in appreciation, and the longer the preacher kept us there each night, the less time there was for fun with our friends after the service. My father thought it over and said, "Penny, if you answer one more altar call we're going to have to take you home to Waxhaw."

At one of those altar calls, I promised to become a missionary and I made the promise in all sincerity. But by the time I was thirteen I had changed my mind. I would serve the God I believe in in other ways. Grandmother assured me that would be all right.

A MAN WITH A mission came to build a new roof for my house. He took deep pride in his work. He was protecting people and their homes, sheltering them from the ravages of wind and rain. To do a good and lasting job, he said, you have to learn to think like water. That's a good system for approaching any problem or challenge.

When I was moving from Dallas, Texas, back home to North Carolina, I met an unforgettable woman with a mission. I hired packers from the moving company to do the laborious job of getting all my worldly goods ready for the long trek back East. To my delight, an ebullient middle-aged lady arrived to do the work. She was a whirlwind of energy and enthusiasm, and she handled my treasures as if they were her own. That was part of her philosophy of moving, she told me. She said, "I love my job. I think I was just born to pack." If we are blessed, we know that feeling—the contentment of believing that we are doing the work we were born to do. And if the daily work of earning a living—Sandburg called it the bread-and-butter job—stands between us and the work we would love to do, we have to find ways to do that work anyway, in some measure. Grab the patchwork quilt scraps of time. Claim that work as an avocation. My mother never earned a penny painting, but she loved to paint in spare moments, and those moments steadied her spirit. Furthermore, the artist in her enriched the sensibilities of the hundreds of students she taught.

Work can be hell, of course, but it can also be joy, sanctuary, salvation. Author Alex Haley used to go to sea to write his books. He had begun writing as a merchant marine, and found the wonderful isolation aboard a freighter at sea a congenial setting for his work as a writer. Some writers can't work against a backdrop of crisis or chaos—just as some bankers, teachers, lawyers, policeman, shoe clerks, or chefs can't. But like most people in any profession, my daughter and I have had to learn to work in spite of everything. For a writer there is respite in the act of writing. We can lose ourselves for many hours in the world of the book—a world over which we have significant power and control. We emerge refreshed to reenter the messy, unruly, chaotic, actual world. We function more effectively in the actual world because we've been able to escape—no matter how briefly—to the relative safe harbor of the world of the book.

Several years ago I spoke to some elementary school students about writing. When I asked for questions, one little girl raised her hand and said, "I've just decided I'm going to be a writer. It sounds like so much more fun than working." I do love my work. Some of it is great fun. But like all work, some of it is difficult, discouraging, frustrating, and exhausting. I wish every person could do work he/she truly loves and enjoys, for this makes the hard parts endurable. But whether I am writing or teaching or speaking or consulting or volunteering, I feel the imprint of Grandmother's work ethic as well as her vision.

Grandmother baked wonderful bread: wholesome, fragrant wheat loaves; crisp corn bread sizzling in an iron skillet blackened by time and countless cooking fires; savory yeast biscuits, light as angel cake and lathered with butter; and fly bread, dense yellow cake heavy laden with fresh blueberries. One summer she gave me lessons in baking bread. Early one morning as we finished mixing the yeast biscuits and set them to rise, she said, "I can give you the recipe and show you the steps. But you really can't do this well unless it's in your hands to do it." This is true of any work. You can know the formula and the routine, but to do any work well, the knack for it has to be in your hands—in your mind and heart and will. You know your true work when you find it: The writer's fingers caress the textures of paper and the shapes of pens; the cabinetmaker's hands find the grain of the wood; the surveyor's eyes and feet decipher the slant of the land toward the creek's rocky bed. My great-nephew Landon Duval fell in love with music when he was not quite two. He could sing—on pitch, on melody—before he could talk. The musicians on both sides of his family pronounced him precocious. One of the first words he learned to say was Vivaldi; actually he called his favorite composer 'Valdi' as he asked to hear the music again. Will music be his vocation? It is love at first sight for many fortunate people when they first encounter their true work.

When you work with a sense of mission, you usually work with a great vision, and you want to do your best to see things through. Sandburg used to pray that God would allow him to live to finish one more book. As he neared the end of that book, he gave thanks that he had survived and he began to pray to live long enough to finish the next one. In a love letter to his wife just before their marriage in 1908, Sandburg wrote, "All the big people are simple, as simple as the unexplored wilderness. They love the universal things that are free to everybody. Light and air and food and love and some work are enough. In the varying phases of these cheap and common things, the great lives have found their joy."

WORK AND A SENSE OF mission can sustain us as we swim alone, and so can love. My father loved his wife, his children, his grandchildren and great-grandchildren, and his fellow man absolutely, unconditionally. He taught me that love is a gift to be given, no strings attached. I knew he loved me no matter what. His was a steady anchor of love that I could always depend on. Some people love conditionally. They give or withhold love, as if love were a commodity to be earned. For some people, love has an omnipresent silent partner—approval. This approval-based love imposes a complicated system of strictures, a kind of Dow Jones barometer of love rising and falling—love given, love withheld. Sometimes you recognize the often-silent signs of disapproval long before you know what you have done, or failed to do.

My father's unswerving love translated into thoughtful action, and many deeds for others were performed quietly and unobtrusively. After he retired, he sat for hours reading in his favorite chair or at his desk. When one of us gave him a book for a gift, he took it as an exchange of trust and read the book faithfully, cover to cover. The books he left on the shelves in his bedroom and den hold a rich legacy: questions and notes he jotted in margins, passages he underlined. Tucked in a book I gave him, I found an old church bulletin on which he had written out a dozen possible titles for my own first book. He read every page of several manuscript drafts of that book, made notes, asked questions. He was a skilled editor and taught me the fundamentals of editing my own work: Go through the text and discard every unnecessary page, he told me. Then go through and throw out every unnecessary paragraph. Next strip out every unnecessary sentence. Then pare every extraneous word.

My father not only adored his children and grandchildren, he respected and fostered their independence and their intellects. This was a special gift to his daughters in the era of our youth. "Be a complete person," he would tell me. "Find your balance and harmony."

When I was a teenager, my aunt Elinor taught me to play the organ so I could serve as organist for the Waxhaw Methodist Church. (Our family monopolized the organ benches in Waxhaw: Aunt Elinor played the organ at the Presbyterian church; Great-aunt Helen was organist at the Baptist church; my sister Lynn succeeded me at the Methodist church organ when I went away to college; Great-aunt Helen's daughter Patsy now plays the organ at the Methodist church.) As I learned to play, my father would slip silently into the sanctuary while I practiced. He had a beautiful voice and was a member of the church choir off and on for more than sixty years. He played the violin—not only favorites from the classical repertoire, but spritely fiddle tunes. He would listen to me at the organ, offering praise or suggesting improvements—usually the latter.

One day he said, "All the notes are right, Penny. But you've got to play with more than right notes." The dancer Martha Graham said to young dancers in training, "You've got to dance with more than your feet." You have to write with more than your head and hands, teach with more than your mind, sell goods with more than your calculator, cultivate a field with more than your tractor, clean house with more than your broom. You pour yourself into your work, infusing it with your spirit as well as your skill.

My father loved and encouraged me even through the sour notes, believing that I truly could play with more than my hands on the organ keyboard and my feet on the pedals. He urged me later on to write with more than words. Swim with more than arms and legs. "If it's worth doing, it's worth doing well," he said, unafraid of a useful platitude. Pour yourself and your love into whatever you are learning to do. Imbue your work with love. My work has never let me down. In work and in human relationships, love is an energy that magically regenerates the more lavishly it is expended.

REAL LOVE. REAL WORK. Real life. A swimmer can feel completely at home in the water—any water—if she is buoyed by real love, real work, real life. As we swim in search of those possibilities, we possess more power to discover them than we realize. Opportunities to love are all around. There is not a single person on this earth who does not need to be loved. Love has as many facets as the most ornately carved gemstone. I love my daughter. I love my family—the blood family I was born into, and my chosen family. I love my son-in-law and the other wonderful people who have married into our family. I love my surrogate children—the sons and daughters I have chosen over the years, and who have chosen me back. I love friends and students and colleagues. There is no romantic love in my life at the moment—unless you count my enduring crushes on Norman Corwin, Cary Grant, Gene Tunney, Gary Cooper, Gregory Peck, Sidney Poitier, and Alan Jackson. But my heart brims with real love of many different varieties for the people who inhabit my life. As one of the children in our family says, a heart always has room to love another person.

I am living a real life and doing real work. I have learned much of my craft because I teach it. In order to teach writing, I have to pare it to its fundamentals, dig into the core of it, find the seeds from which it grows. My students have taught me many vital lessons in return. The best single thing I have ever heard anyone anywhere say about writing was uttered by one of my students.

He was repeating his sophomore year in high school and I had taught high school English for two years, so we should have been evenly matched. He had the edge in authority, though. To his peers, his word was law. He was the leader of a preeminent gang in the area. I was just a teacher, and a woman at that. Fortunately, our class convened after lunch, and this student—we'll call him Roy— usually settled into his desk in the front row and immediately went to sleep. (He was a young man of hefty appetite and rumor had it that he routinely ate three or four lunches—his own and the lunches he coerced from other students.)

I felt more comfortable with Roy asleep than Roy awake, and, in September, his classmates and I tried not to disturb him. The class and I simply communicated in hushed voices so we wouldn't wake him up. But by October I felt more in command, and Roy's slumbers became something of an affront. One day I woke him up and said, "Roy, you should hear this."

"Why?" he wanted to know. "Will it help me in life? I don't want to hear nothing that won't help me in life."

Roy had a point. Indeed he was entitled to hear what would help him in life. Life is too short to listen to things that won't help us in life. We struck a bargain that day. I would tell him and his classmates honestly whether the day's lesson would truly be likely to help them in life, or whether the state and local curriculum committees just thought it would. Roy could count on my word, and I could count on his. If the lesson had no relevance to Roy's life, Roy was free to sleep. In the interest of parity, I extended the option to my other students as well, but they were by then accustomed to trying obediently to learn what was set out before them, whether it was helpful or not.

It was real learning for real life Roy wanted, and I tried from then on not to waste a minute of time on meaningless matter, trivial ideas, irrelevance, and rote emptiness. I wanted to honor Roy's right to real learning for real life. I wanted to honor those rights for every student I taught—and for myself.

I slipped up now and then, of course, but Roy made me toe the line. As I gave a composition assignment one day, Roy—wide awake—threw his pencil on his desk. "I am not doing that assignment," he said indignantly. "You're asking me to do fake writing. Real writing is hard enough. I'm not about to do any fake writing."

His wisdom stunned me, and I have never forgotten it. I keep Roy's words nearby, and I share them with other writers to this day. Real writing is hard enough indeed. I don't want to write fake writing; I don't want to read fake writing.

Roy set me straight about real writing and real life. Lucy Kroll taught me not to tell myself no. I'll never learn to swim alone if I tell myself I can't. I'll never write a book (substitute your own aspirations here) if I tell myself I can't. Nobody is likely to knock on my door and say, "Is there anybody in there who would like to write a book?" I am going to have to swim alone, write alone, and face the possibility of rejection and failure alone. I might as well tell myself yes. I will leave it to others to tell me no—and I may pay them no attention at all.

PART OF SWIMMING alone is working at swimming better alone. My first editor, Robert Stewart, taught me the joys of Re-vision. He taught me to dig into my manuscript and to cut, hone, refine, polish, burnish. With Robert as my tutor, I learned to love revising, and to find it an intensely creative stage in the writing process. I am a multidraft writer. I never get a manuscript even close to where it needs to be in the first draft. I don't count the drafts anymore. I keep on revising until someone takes the manuscript away from me. As Sandburg said, you never finish writing a biography. You just have to know when to stop.

As Robert used to tell me, I tell my students in turn that, except for unequivocal standards of language usage, they may choose to ignore my editing notes. "Your name is on the title page," he'd say. "You own the text." For better or worse, I am in charge. Swimming alone, I am ultimately responsible for my book, myself, my life.

Life, like a manuscript, can be enhanced by periodic re-visioning—rethinking, reshaping, reordering, reconfiguring. When you revise a manuscript—or, in some cases, a life—don't disparage or denigrate what came earlier. Don't say, "I can't believe I wrote it that way. How perfectly awful!" Most likely, you wrote it the best way you could at the time. That draft helped to get you where you are now and where you are going to go.

Sometimes a swimmer actually has to change direction in the water—to change lifestyles, to change jobs, to change goals. Consequently, a wise swimmer learns how to change direction in mid-swim—how to turn her body in a wide semicircle through the water; how to reach her arms toward the new direction she has chosen. *Turn your head in the direction you wish to go, and your shoulders and hips will follow. Kick forcefully to keep your body high in the water as you turn.*

Whether I am staying the course or changing directions, one of my highest goals as a swimmer is to feel at home in the water. Before I can feel at home in the water, I have to learn to feel at home within myself. When I am at home within myself, I am at home anywhere—everywhere.

I HAVE TO BE ABLE to swim alone, even though, I am told, it is wiser for me not to do so. *Try not to swim alone. Try to swim with someone who can help you or get help if there is an emergency.* What kind of sense does that make? Swim alone, but don't? The point is, that for a list of compelling reasons, I need to be self-sufficient enough to swim alone, to feel at home in the water, and to feel at ease with my capacity to handle emergencies. But I do not always have to swim alone. Once, as I fretted over a writing deadline, my father said, "No. It's not a deadline. It's a lifeline." We swimmers need lifelines to ensure our safety and to connect us to shore. However, I should not have to be isolated. I need—I deserve to have someone with me who can either help me or get help for me if there is an emergency.

I come from proud, independent folk. We bend way over backward to try to do everything ourselves. We hate to impose, to intrude, to ask for help. We are adept at improvising, coping, making do. As one incensed friend said to one of us struggling valiantly, if foolishly, to deal with a crisis alone, "When you don't let us help you, you deprive those of us who love you of the chance to love you enough."

Let other swimmers help you. In turn, reach out to other swimmers—not only those in need of rescuing, but those who may simply need encouraging, affirming, cheering on. When the inevitable emergencies happen, know that you come to them equipped with skills developed over a lifetime of swimming. Rely on your experience, your creative ways of coping with crisis. Rely on who you are, what you know how to do, what you can learn how to do, and what you can figure out on the spot and improvise.

For the past nine years our family has been swimming upstream coping with health emergencies. At one time both our parents were in the hospital, critically ill. The three Niven sisters, Penny, Lynn, and Doris, spent so much time in the hospital that we were sometimes mistaken for employees. We devised the following strategies for coping with an ongoing series of health emergencies:

1. *Be a team.* We send up big, vociferous prayers, as well as prayers of gratitude. We work together as a formidable team. In one hospital, nurses and even doctors quickly realized it was simpler to answer our questions and respond to our concerns than to deal with the repercussions of an encounter with any unhappy Nivens.

2. *Listen and learn.* We listen to the answers and diagnoses we are given. We ask more questions and gather more answers. Then we aggressively research the illness, the condition, and the standard and state-of-the-art treatments and treatment facilities. We find the experts and consult them. Only the best care will do.

3. *Serve as advocates.* Once we have gathered all the information our brains can hold, we take a stand. We say our piece. We have spoken on behalf of our parents—and others—who can't or won't speak for themselves. We share the outcome of our research and experience. We write letters of complaint, and we write letters of appreciation. It is just as important to praise the positives in an experience as it is to protest the negatives.

4. *Hang on to a sense of humor.* We learned a long time ago that laughter is a powerful leavening force. A sense of humor is a vital survival skill. So we let ourselves laugh at the inevitable comedies interwoven into the emergencies. Our mother, even in the throes of a heart attack and its aftermath, was very particular about her surroundings. She objected to the decorative border rimming the ceiling of her hospital room. She asked to have pictures on the wall straightened or removed altogether. She tried to interest young physicians and

chaplains in courting her unmarried daughters, despite the fact that we were easily twice as old as the physicians and chaplains (most of whom, it seemed to me, were barely out of their teens). During one of their simultaneous hospital sojourns, my parents sent me running between their separate rooms on separate floors, the messenger as they continued their perennial debate over being cremated versus being embalmed. Daddy was all for cremation, which Mamma viewed disapprovingly as radical, unorthodox, and unseemly.

"What will people think?" she wanted to know.

"I don't care what people think," our father replied. "I won't be here to listen to their opinions." He was going to be cremated, he announced, and that was that.

"Well, I can't decide," Mamma said at last. "I'll just leave it up to you children."

"Suppose we can't decide?" my brother Bill responded. "Shall we just compromise and have half of you embalmed and the other half cremated?" He is the only son and he has always gotten away with such impertinence, but even Mamma laughed at the bizarre image.

We had been afraid that our elderly parents were doing to die. Suddenly they had rallied enough to sit up in their hospital beds and feud about the ultimate disposition of their bodies. They were going to survive. It takes enormous energy to be that feisty and contrary. Where there is humor there is hope.

5. *Love each other through the emergency.* Sometimes, after you have tried every possible action, the emergency defies your best efforts. All you can do then is love each other through the ordeal. When she was asked how we coped with one particular illness and death, Jennifer said, "We just loved each other through it."

IF YOU LOVE AND TRUST the Power of the Water, you never actually swim alone. There are many names for God. Each swimmer ultimately has to find her way to her own view of Alpha and Omega, the beginning and the end, the first and the last. A child once said to a friend of mine, "Your God must be a heart." What force beats in the mystic heart of life? What infinite source of life flows through each of us, every living creature?

The longer I live, the more I learn, and the farther I swim, the more I trust the Power of the Water. This Power far beyond my own enfolds me, supports me, propels me, and sustains me. As a writer, I see the world metaphorically. I examine the sacred texts of several religions for the metaphors for God inscribed there. Creator. Father. Teacher. King. Protector. Avenger. Judge. Friend. Spirit. When I try to comprehend some of the awful tragedies that beset the creatures of this earth, I turn to the metaphor of the father, the parent. This parent metaphor leads me to think of my immense, infinite love for my own child. I would give anything I am and have to protect and shield her. Yet I cannot protect her from all danger and shield her from all suffering. What I can do is love her, comfort her, be present to her, and trust and affirm her own grace and strength. I find solace in the timeless, holy metaphor of the parent.

Swimming through the murkiest waters over great, hard distances, I swim buoyed by the Power of the Water—the "Power Whose Center Is Everywhere." I feel palpable love and comfort. There is a steady presence that has never left me—although from time to time, I have pulled away, only to come gratefully home again. I swim enfolded in love, mystery, trust, and hope. When I doubt my own strength I float or tread water or rest on the glide. Then I swim on, free and secure in the knowledge that whether I am one swimmer in the water or one of many, I never swim alone.

SWIMMING PRACTICE

Swimming Lesson Nine:
Swimming Alone

1. Write about what Martha Graham called your unique expression, using the prompt: "There is only one of me in all time. I am unique because _____."

2. Think about what work means to you and list at least five words that come to mind when you think about your work. Use the following prompt: "Work means _____."

3. What does real love mean to you? Write about it; or paint or draw a picture of it; or create or choose a poem, some music, a photograph or some other visual image that expresses your vision of real love.

4. Are you thinking about changing directions in the water—changing lifestyle, jobs, goals, or relationships? Apply the debate queries given for Swimming Lesson Six as you make a rough map of where you are and where you want to be. Map out visually or write about this possible change of direction, using the three prompts that debaters use:

    A. "It is necessary (or not necessary) to do this because _____."

    B. "It is desirable (or not desirable) to do this because _____."

    C. "It is feasible (or not feasible) to do this because _____."

5. Jot down a list of your lifelines—the people, the circumstances, the possibilities—and explain why these are lifelines for you. Make a list of people or circumstances that you serve as a lifeline, and why or how you do.

6. Write your own definition of the Power of the Water.

X. Swimming in the Ocean

*Get to know the water where you plan to swim.
Look out for hidden dangers beneath the surface
that may not be apparent from above or from the
shore. Know the rhythm of the tides, the flow of the
currents, and the outlook for the weather. Then you
can dive into the ocean and swim toward new
horizons.*

I N JUNE Jennifer, Coddy Granum, and I went to Duck, North Carolina, on the Outer Banks, seeking rest and respite from the daily hubbub. Needing to breathe, needing to float, I swam with pleasure in the landlocked swimming pool near our rented cottage. On its surface, the Atlantic Ocean was placid that week, but, wary of rip tides and jellyfish, I chose not to swim in the ocean. To my fascination others did: fathers and children; teenage boys; an exuberant Labrador retriever who foisted his Frisbee on friends and strangers alike, time after time swimming through the surf to retrieve it for someone else to toss it on an outgoing wave. At about noon each day, far out toward the horizon, a swimmer came into view heading north, plowing up the coast with strength, skill, and a powerful rhythm.

Every swimmer brings his own aspirations and needs to the ocean, his own perceptions of "the wonders in the deep," as Psalm 107 describes the "great waters." Swimming in the ocean can mean venturing into the wonders of new landscapes, of new cities or countries. It can mean living as a responsible citizen in the world you inhabit.

Swimming in the ocean can mean navigating the interior universe, the inner life of mind and spirit—Thoreau's "Atlantic and Pacific Ocean of one's being alone."

Swimming in the ocean can mean confronting mortality and contemplating whatever world lies beyond this one—the world for which death is the threshold. In *Moby-Dick,* Herman Melville writes, "There is one knows not what sweet mystery about this sea, whose gently awful stirrings seem to speak of some hidden soul beneath." Swimming in the ocean can mean exploring the "sweet mystery," the "hidden soul" in the universe.

No matter the destination, the purpose, or the prospect of reward, swimming in the ocean requires a certain knowledge, a keen awareness of hidden dangers, and a profound respect for the tides, the currents, and the weather. So armed, you can begin your journey, real or imagined. You can swim in the ocean in body, in mind, and in spirit. Do you actually yearn to travel or even to move to a new place? Do you alternately dread and then long to dive into the depths of your inner life in the quest to know who you are and who you are becoming? Do you find yourself confronting the prospects of aging and mortality? Each of these journeys may take you to the brink of an ocean and the moment when you have to decide if you want to swim.

Some swimmers yearn for the primal freedom and promise of the open sea, despite the perils that may lurk in the depths. Other lives are lived richly in estuaries, lakes, rivers, or streams, bodies of water that can be boundless or constricting, depending on circumstances and point of view. For Great-aunt Geneva Walkup Rone, Waxhaw, North Carolina, was the hub of the universe—the only body of water worth swimming and the yardstick by which life in every other place on earth was to be measured.

Hadn't her great-great-great-great-great grandfather traveled from Ireland to find freedom and help settle the Waxhaws? Hadn't he built his house and farmed his land with his own hands? Hadn't he fought the British for his home and freedom during the Revolutionary War? Back in 1767, hadn't one of Geneva's ancestors in the Waxhaws Settlement had the presence of mind to go over to Sarah Jackson's cabin when her time had come to help midwife her baby Andrew into the world, so he could grow up and become the seventh president of the United States of America, once there was a United States?

We often say that Andrew Jackson was born in Waxhaw and nothing much has happened there since. Actually, everything of fundamental importance has happened there—love, birth, life, death. As far as Aunt Genny was concerned, you didn't have to leave Waxhaw to find all you could want or need in a lifetime. On Aunt Genny's map of the world there were just four places. Heaven. Hell. Waxhaw. And Off Somewhere. If you knew what was good for you, you were working zealously, moment by moment, to get yourself to Heaven. And one way to do that was to stay in Waxhaw. Going Off Somewhere usually meant trouble: opportunities to sin in expensive department stores, bars, saloons, or houses of ill repute. Sometimes it was the trouble of daily deprivation and inconvenience—the difficulty, for instance, of procuring self-rising flour in Pennsylvania.

I married a man from Off Somewhere—from Charlotte, more than twenty miles up Providence Road from Waxhaw. He planned to take me to live even further Off Somewhere—in Philadelphia, where he would go to graduate school. (As one of my relatives saw it, Jack was going to get his doctorate, but it seemed like a waste of time since he wouldn't be allowed to write prescriptions.) Before we moved, Aunt Genny saw to it that I was equipped with all the best family recipes—*her* recipes.

After Jack and I settled into our new lives Off Somewhere, I decided to bake Aunt Genny's famous Featherlight Yeast Rolls. Her recipe called for self-rising flour, one of the few convenient modern shortcuts that old-fashioned Southern cooks allowed on their pantry shelves. Off to the market I went. No self-rising flour. I checked another grocery nearby. Still no luck. There were hundreds of grocery stores in the Philadelphia metropolitan area, and I had canvassed only two. But I missed Aunt Genny and everyone else back in Waxhaw, and I thought I'd surprise her with a long distance phone call. While I was at it, I would ask her how much baking powder to add to regular flour if self-rising flour wasn't handy. She'd be pleased.

What she was was horrified—first at the scare my call

gave her, for long distance usually meant bad news; then at the extravagance of it since there was no heart-stopping emergency to justify a long distance call; and finally, at the news that Pennsylvania did not have self-rising flour. She was appalled, but not one bit surprised. That's what you got for going Off Somewhere.

Some people have no need or desire to swim in the ocean. Aunt Genny was one of those. She found everything she loved and desired in Waxhaw, including her husband, Uncle Sam Rone, who had the good sense to move *to* Waxhaw from Off Somewhere. He worked in the drug store, fell in love with Aunt Genny, and courted and married her. It was a late marriage for both of them and the first for each. They settled down happily to live with Aunt Genny's mother, Great-grandmother Walkup, in her old house next door to the Methodist church. Aunt Genny was a pillar of the church, the Sunday school, and the ladies' circle. She never had any children of her own, and we were blessed that she filled that void in her life by lavishing her love, and her cooking, on us. In her kitchen, and Grandmother Ellen's and Grandmother Penelope's, I learned that cooking can be sacramental: To love people is to cook for them and with them, to feed them, to nourish them, to sustain their very lives.

Aunt Genny stayed in one place, living the universal in the particular, as Thornton Wilder said of characters in his plays, finding the "cosmic in the commonplace." Waxhaw was all the ocean she needed or wanted. Others of us in the family struck out to swim in new and distant waters, venturing into the ocean, seeking the particular in the universal, hoping to find ourselves in the journey.

AS YOU SWIM in "the Atlantic and Pacific Ocean of one's being alone," you tackle an introspective journey into the mind and spirit. You confront the mysterious, boundless depths that have captivated and confounded countless swimmers since time began.

When I was much younger, I used to read with shivery fascination about lonely, courageous heroes who were imprisoned in solitary confinement in remote dungeon cells, left alone with the rats, the damp, and the bread crusts, and only their thoughts for company. Whatever the reason for their imprisonment, whether the punishment was just or cruel, these heroes took with them into the dungeons one common blessing: Each seemed to possess a well-nourished mind. One man could sustain within his own head a debate on the deepest philosophical issues. Another could recite poetry for hours on end. The well-nourished mind could withstand the rigors of bread and water, scurrying rats, mold, and threats of torture. I used to wonder if, given similar circumstances, I could fare as well. I feared not. The poems I had memorized ran to Ernest Thayer's "Casey at the Bat," Rudyard Kipling's "If," Joyce Kilmer's "Trees," and various ditties by Edgar A. Guest. After a few days of reciting "It takes a heap o' livin' in a house t' make it home," I suspected I would find the rats more interesting than the poetry.

Nourishing the mind is imperative for growth and survival, whether you are swimming in the vast waters of the ocean or the sheltered waters of a lake or pool. A well-nourished mind is a requisite for a full, rich, and happy life. The CBS News journalist Charles Kuralt discovered an elderly black sharecropper in the deep South who, deprived of a conventional education, schooled himself out of a sheer love of learning. He had collected a huge secondhand library, which was destroyed by fire. When Kuralt notified his television audience of the man's loss, thousands of volumes poured in to the self-appointed scholar, who had said his aspiration was "to wage war on my ignorance." This is a noble purpose for a lifetime.

In one of his notebooks, Leonardo da Vinci spoke about the well-nourished mind: "The knowledge of past times and of the places of the earth is both an ornament and nutriment to the human mind . . . Learning acquired in youth arrests the evil of old age; and if you understand that old age has wisdom for its food, you will so conduct yourself in youth that your old age will not lack for nourishment."

The well-nourished mind is a key, I think, to the vitality that belies calendar years. This has been true of the people I admire who have lived to great age. I have vicariously inhabited the well-nourished minds of the elders in my family, and the elders in my books. My father was vibrantly alive, despite the physical frailties that ultimately did him in. At the end of her life, my mother's body was beset with problems, and, nearing eighty-six, she had little short-term memory; but her long-term memory kept going strong. Even in hospice care, she was the authoritative, meticulous school teacher, correcting the grammar of family members, nurses, doctors, chaplains, volunteers, and visitors galore. One day when we thought death was very close by, my brother stepped into our mother's room and spoke a quiet hello.

"Is that you, Bill?" Mamma asked in a whisper.

"Yes, Mamma, it's me," he replied.

Suddenly her voice became clear and emphatic. "No, Bill," she reprimanded. "Don't say, 'It's me.' Say 'It is *I.*'"

After she had corrected a visitor's grammar another day, my mother vowed, "If it's the last thing I do, I am going to teach people how to use *lie* and *lay.*"

We knew her life was ebbing away. All the more reason to applaud that words still mattered, that the instinct to teach and parent held strong. All the more reason to celebrate that she could still say adamantly, "It is *I.*"

I USED TO THINK there was an Ocean of Life and an Ocean of Death. As I grow older I see that they are the same—an entity, a unity in a great cosmic cycle. We learned about birth and death early on and firsthand in Waxhaw. The seasons of life are deeply personal in a town of eight hundred people. I suppose my generation was the last to learn about death before television came along to demystify and depersonalize it—to show us death and violence as entertainment, dehumanizing and trivializing the reality in the process. Movies and television give us graphic, gratuitous, generic death. In Waxhaw, each death had a name and a face. Death brought real grief and real loss to real people you knew and cared about. And you grew up understanding that death is a season, an inevitable destination in the cycle of life. You also grew up knowing where you would most likely be buried, and whose family plots adjoined your own. People in Waxhaw usually died at home, surrounded by people who loved them. As if it were a cosmic relay race, the body's journey from the deathbed to the grave was transacted personally. The shell that had contained the life was entrusted to the familiar hands of relatives, friends, the town doctor, the mortician, the gravedigger, and the minister.

Death is not a prospect I fear. I'd just as soon live on zestfully, vigorously, for a long time yet. But I am not afraid to die, anymore than I was afraid to enter puberty, or give birth, or go through menopause. These are seasons, journeys as ancient as time and being. To live is to experience these journeys. Saint-Exupéry wrote in *Flight to Arras,* "To live is to be slowly born." And to slowly die. The secret is to let the birthing and growing supersede the dying.

According to the story, as Henry David Thoreau lay on his deathbed, he was asked if he had made his peace with God. He replied, "I did not know we had ever quarreled..." My father did not, as far as I can tell, ever quarrel with God. He certainly did not do so within my memory. My father knew that in certain matters he had erred—sometimes by choice, sometimes not—but he never presumed to quarrel with God. He was very sure about God's expectations.

As my father swam in the ocean in the last years of his long life, he probed the "sweet mystery," reading widely, and studying the Bible and certain other theological texts. He carried on an occasional dialogue with Elton Trueblood, the great Quaker theologian, who lived at Earlham College while we were there. My father questioned, to be sure, but more out of a scrupulous desire to understand than out of challenge. He lived his convictions and turned his brilliant mind with unswerving humility toward universal questions. More than anyone I have ever known, he tried, especially in his later years, to live his beliefs, every day, in every human relationship. He was constantly being born—not being born again, in a religious sense—but being born to new insights, new wisdom, new planes of enlightenment. Day by day, my father made his peace with life, and so with death.

More than three years after his death I am still hearing stories about his life, from family, friends, and strangers. They fall into two major categories: mischief and good deeds. The good deeds were done quietly, most often kept secret between my father and the recipient. The mischief usually involved our mother, whom our father loved to tease, or one of his Niven relatives or in-laws. Once he was in charge of ordering a tombstone for a family member's grave. A thrifty man, he did his usual comparison shopping, and found a tombstone two-for-one sale. Buy one, get one free. It was nearing time for our mother's birthday, and Daddy told us gleefully that he thought he'd take advantage of that two-for-one sale and give Mamma the other tombstone for her birthday. Was he teasing or not? Sometimes we couldn't be certain, so we made him swear not to buy that tombstone for a birthday gift, and he didn't.

For years, my father and our cousin, Don Murray, regularly traveled in their work, and often found themselves in the same hotel in the same Carolina town. They loved people, and loved to sing, and Daddy loved to play his fiddle. At the end of a day's work, the two travelers would be drawn to the cheerful hubbub of any party or convention going on in their hotel. A funeral director told me the story of my father's unsuccessful endeavors to get himself invited to the banquet for a convention of morticians. At the banquet the funeral director glanced at the orchestra playing in the background, and there was my father, fiddling away in the violin section. Don and Daddy eventually devised an ingenious plan that was so successful they never had to crash another party or convention: They bought fancy beribboned badges that read "HOST" in bold letters. Their host badges admitted them to every event in every hotel from that time on. Often, at the end of a festive evening, they stood at the door so that departing guests could express appreciation for their hospitality. Don died two years after Daddy, and I can picture them at the Pearly Gates wearing their host badges, welcoming new arrivals.

My father enjoyed quoting Robert Frost's ditty: "Forgive, O Lord, my little jokes on Thee, and I'll forgive Thy great big joke on me." He sometimes celebrated and sometimes deplored the human foibles that often define marriages, organized religion, and politics—international, national, and grass-roots. Yet he stressed that we were never to speak an unkind word about another person, especially in anger. "If you can't say something kind, say nothing at all," he would admonish. On occasion, however, and always with just cause, he did find it necessary to speak critically of certain politicians—and certain referees officiating at University of North Carolina basketball games.

Our father ingrained in us our responsibility to vote, to work where we are to make things better, and to walk sympathetically in other people's shoes. He spoke and wrote his pride in all of us. "My children and grandchildren are beautiful and brilliant," he would say. "But if they had been ugly and dumb, I would have loved them anyway." And he would have. He wrote this letter to us on Father's Day in 1990:

It's an almost insurmountable challenge to merit the love and deep caring of a wife who has survived fifty-two years of striving and loving; of four over-achieving, superior, outstanding, role model, indescribable children; of five multitalented, beautiful, worldly-wise, and unblemished grandchildren who will make the world a much better habitat. If this won't humble one, try plowing a

stubborn mule on July 4th in corn over head high
and always downwind.

CARING FOR ELDERLY parents abruptly brings you face to
face with their mortality and your own. As I watched my
father and mother struggle against the daunting tides of illness and old age, I realized that there is a significant difference between getting older and growing older. Some
people just passively get older, falling into old age as if
falling asleep. Some people keep growing all their lives.
My parents grew older, and kept on growing. Even in my
father's last years, in his senescence, there was a sweet
nobility in his manner, a refined elegance of mind and
spirit, as if he had been sanctified. His wit stayed; and
even as senile dementia robbed him of his comprehen-
sion of many common things, he beheld the world with
an original vision that was sometimes startling in its irony.
One day I came upon this most peaceful of men sitting
transfixed before a violent television movie—something
he would never have watched in earlier years. He turned
to me, smiled, shook his head and said, "Makes you glad
you're out here and not in there."

In the last few months of his life, aphasia took my father's considerable language skills away for hours, even
days, at a time. When he couldn't find the words he
wanted to speak, he invented delightful words, melliflu-
ous, multisyllabic words, uttered with such authority and
eloquence that it didn't matter that they made no sense

whatsoever to us. We listened, enchanted, and responded with appreciation. Finally, those words escaped him as well.

As time goes on, a victim of senile dementia or Alzheimer's disease usually reverts to his native language. My father's native language, it turns out, was music, expressed with his beautiful voice and his gifted hands on the violin. In the end, that language did not fail him. His lips would tremble in the futile effort to summon the words to speak to us, and then, thwarted, he would turn to music. He sang to and about his wife and children, his grandchildren, nurses, and caregivers. He composed the words and the melody as he went along. He was singing to us across worlds, across oceans—singing his vision of the world he was approaching and his legacy to the world he was leaving behind. When he had no words left to speak, he sang his love for people, and for life and time. One of his last songs went this way:

I love this world.
I love every minute I've spent in this world.
Even the hard times were good.
I love my wife and my children.
I have always tried to take care of them and to
*   love them.*
I love the grandchildren and the newborn
*   children.*
I love all my children. They will be wild angels
*   again.*

Wild angels. Unruly, unfettered, audacious, unconventional angels. At the Greek root, *angelos,* the angel is a messenger. As a messenger, an angel becomes an instrument. Whether we believe in literal angels or not, whether we swim in the ocean or in the local pool, all of us are messengers and instruments—for bad or good, worse or better, sorrow or joy, stagnation or growth, despair or hope.

When my father sang about his children reverting to wild angelhood, I doubt he was thinking of the four major archangels who appear in the sacred texts of Judaism, Christianity, and Islam: the chief archangel, Michael, the protector and the Prince of Light; Gabriel, the archangel of revelation, rescue, and new beginnings; gentle Raphael, the archangel of healing; and Uriel, the archangel of knowledge, creativity, and retribution. I doubt my father was thinking of the cherubim and seraphim, or the principalities and powers.

I suspect the wild angels he envisioned are metaphorical more than miraculous—not the conventional radiant, winged angels of scriptures, classical literature, and religious art, but the unconventional angels who serve as messengers and instruments in daily life. My father was such an angel. My daughter is a sturdy, luminous angel. People flock like moths to her light. Lucy Kroll was an angel in the form of a mentor and agent who transformed my creative life—or enabled me to transform it. Grandmother Ellen was a healing angel, a teaching angel.

I could call a long roll of unconventional angels— family members, friends, and strangers, some of them mysterious. There was the one-armed flower lady on Oki-nawa who appeared out of nowhere on Jennifer's first Christmas Eve. A knock on the door, and there she stood, offering one beautiful Christmas wreath for sale. I had been longing in vain for such a wreath. We had never seen this flower lady before and we never saw her again. There was the taxi driver with whom I shared a prolonged Manhattan traffic jam the year after my divorce. We discovered that he and my mother had the same birthday and his mother and I shared the same birthday. "Here's my philosophy of life," he told me. "Love. Trust. And don't look back." His name was Feight—pronounced Fate.

There is the man who has coached hundreds of inner-city boys on basketball courts, real and makeshift. He has also taken them to summer camp, lectured them about their manners and their homework, set them on the path to college, and helped them and their parents find jobs. There are the neighbors who come to your door and my door with casseroles, soup, pies, cakes, and flowers, to ease the hard times. There is the angel patron who reaches out anonymously to help young, struggling writers. There are the nurses, nursing assistants, doctors, social workers, chaplains, and volunteers who cared for our parents at Aldersgate in Charlotte, North Carolina.

As I swim, I often bump into angels who come to the rescue, who encourage me to keep treading water, keep swimming, keep diving. Sometimes they keep me company, these wild angels. And because my father expected me to be a wild angel, I will do my best to comply. I cherish this enduring legacy of love and wisdom, and I keep striving to live up to it.

I understand that my father was nearly eighty-six and suffering when he died. I was, after all, nearly sixty-one myself, a woman grown and still growing. I understand that Olin Niven lived a long, full life, and that he had been ebbing away, and that it was time to let him go. But in my heart somewhere I am six years old, and I want my daddy to come home.

Since the death of Jennifer's father, I often picture her when she was three and he was overseas. All those long ago afternoons, as suppertime neared, Jennifer perched hopefully on the front steps, waiting for her daddy to come home from Vietnam. We keep each other company, my daughter and I, perched on the steps of memory, missing our fathers, loving them in the deepest chambers of our hearts, wishing them home again.

GRIEF FOR THOSE who have died ebbs and flows like the ocean tide—except without a predictable rhythm. Sometimes it swamps me, takes me by surprise. Other times I can see it coming. But there is peace, and I find deeper and deeper solace through that peace and through time, along with the growing belief that what we love most in another person becomes an eternal part of us.

Since my father's death, as has been true all my life, I have felt his steady loving presence. I feel it now, every day. As I always have, I talk to him in my head. I miss his impromptu midday long-distance telephone calls—an extravagance for a frugal man. Because Mamma loved to talk on the telephone, Daddy got to speak very few words when the three of us were chatting long distance. So he called, just for a moment, when my mother was out and about, to ask how I truly was, and to tell me he loved me.

Not long ago, two people broke into our family home place, the house in the Waxhaw countryside where our parents lived for more than twenty years, and where my brother now makes his home. The house had never before been invaded and robbed. We installed an alarm system immediately, bemoaning the loss of innocence and trust that even Waxhaw can't escape. Troubles previously associated with Off Somewhere are hitting home.

Among other possessions, the thieves stole our father's Seth Thomas grandmother clock and his violin. Five generations of our family heard my father play his violin. Woven into most of the Christmases of my life are memories of the music Daddy made on the violin with one of us at the organ or piano and everyone singing "Silent night, holy night, All is calm; all is bright...."

My hope is that whoever stole my father's violin urgently needed to make music or to give it to someone else who needed to make music. I can't bear to think it was stolen to be pawned or sold for something as meaningless as money. And if it was money that was needed, my father would have listened and most likely provided it, as he did to many others, as a gift or a loan, to be worked off with honest chores around the home place.

We treasured that violin. "How much was it worth?" the insurance agent asked. "Priceless," we answered. "Irreplaceable."

It took us some time to realize that the thieves stole the violin but not the music. The violin, in the end, was only old wood and strings. The music lived in our father. The music lives in us. We will always keep the music.

OUR MOTHER DIED peacefully on March 23, 2003. My sister and my niece were with her, and so was a nurse named Comfort. I had just finished the first draft of this book, and had read passages to my mother along the way. As always, she listened intently, her blue eyes bright with questions, interest, and pride. As I worked on the subsequent drafts, I longed for the steady encouragement she gave me. It was not easy, as I revised, to convert the passages about my mother to the past tense; but the act of doing so ultimately yielded revelations about how much of her essence defies boundaries of time and space.

Our mother had at least nine lives; beginning with her first heart attack, she flirted with the boundaries of life and death. Her steely, stubborn strength defied the gloomy predictions of several doctors and nurses. She held on to life fiercely—for life itself, but most of all, for us. She suffered a grave illness before Jennifer's first book was published, but rallied, determined, as she said, to hold Jennifer's book in her hands, and she did. She was absolutely determined to be here: for our father during his illness; for family weddings and birthdays; for the birth of her great-grandchildren. The eighth, Emma, was born three days before my mother died. She knew about Emma's arrival, asked her name, and gave the name her blessing.

My mother's passion for life extended to its smallest details—from the fine points of grammar to the decoration of the Christmas tree to the manners of the hummingbirds she invited to the glass feeders mounted just outside the screen porch. She mixed the sweet, red juice for the hummingbird feeders with a bountiful hand and the same care she gave to preparing a meal for family and friends. The hummingbirds darted around the feast in droves, tiny wings whirring, dive-bombing each other, greedy for exclusive rights to the nectar shimmering in the glass.

Our mother could chastise her children or grandchildren with a withering look when they failed to share or play together in harmony; but stern glances alone could not deter these deceptively delicate little birds. To no avail, she tried rattling the screen porch door or waving a broomstick to establish order. One summer day we heard Mamma say to the hummingbirds, "There is plenty of nectar to go around. If you cannot learn to share, I'm just going to bring these feeders inside." They didn't, and she did.

Lessons in good manners for hummingbirds and children. Lessons in grammar and grace. Lessons in holding on, surviving in the great ocean of life.

My mother was at once a conventional Southern lady and a free spirit. That dichotomy explained her indecision about cremation, and, as she had abdicated the decision, we chose cremation. Our father traveled so widely and constantly during his career that he was profoundly glad to come home to Waxhaw to stay. There was no question that all his ashes should be buried in the Waxhaw cemetery where his parents and sister, his grandparents and great-grandparents, two of his sons-in-law, and many of his other relatives and friends are buried. There was no question that he and our mother would be buried together, and now they are. But our mother was Waxhaw-bound for so many years of her life that I wanted to take some of her ashes to places she loved beyond Waxhaw— the ocean; the mountains; Marshville, her childhood home. In the Blue Ridge Mountains in North Carolina, I have climbed a sun-laced trail, bordered by lush ferns, to scatter some of my mother's ashes. Through the deep woods there is a glimpse of other hills, of a clear mountain lake and a waterfall. At sunset one summer day on the Outer Banks, Jennifer, our dear friend, Coddy, and I walked the quiet beach to celebrate the lives of my mother, Jennifer's father, and Coddy's mother, all deceased within months of each other. We read poetry, and then we entrusted a portion of Eleanor Marsh Hearon Niven's ashes to the ocean.

"In its mysterious past," Rachel Carson wrote in *The Sea Around Us,* "[the sea] encompasses all the dim origins of life and receives in the end, after, it may be, many transmutations, the dead husks of that same life. For all at last return to the sea—to Oceanus, the ocean river, like the everflowing stream of time, the beginning and the end."

AT TIMES I FEEL about swimming in the ocean as Stephen Crane wrote about sailing in "The Open Boat": "A singular disadvantage of the sea lies in the fact that after successfully surmounting one wave you discover that there is another behind it just as important and just as nervously anxious to do something effecting in the way of swamping boats."

Swimming in the ocean requires constant vigilance; even with that we may be swamped. More than ever, we need to learn when to float, when to tread water, and how to find and hold on to the upward force. We need not be timid or negligent about exploring the private seas of the soul, mind, and heart. We can master the strokes that enable us to swim with our heads up. Then we can truly see our fellow swimmers in the ocean and communicate with them fruitfully as we swim toward Tomorrow, as we give Tomorrow its shape and substance.

My swimming heroine, Esther Williams, writes about two narrow escapes from drowning in the ocean. She was ten years old, and already a good swimmer, the morning that she and her brother set out on a practice swim in the ocean waters off Hermosa Beach in California. All of a sudden she was caught in a wall of rough waves but her brother pulled her to safety. Many years later, while she and a friend were swimming in the ocean waters off Acapulco, they were sucked into a whirlpool near the mouth of a river feeding into the sea. The two swimmers fought their way out of the whirlpool and then gave themselves up to the tide, riding it down shore to the beach.

"Let the tide carry you when you can't escape it," Esther Williams writes. "Swim at a relaxed pace with the current, but on the diagonal to it. In doing this you will be able to direct yourself in the general direction you wish to go without actually fighting the current." Pay attention to Esther: Don't struggle against the current. Learn to ride it so that it takes you where you want to go. But swim against the tide if you have to, seeking the destination you choose. Let purpose, not expediency, set your course.

Don't take foolish risks in rough, choppy ocean waters—but do not let fear keep you from the joy of a buoyant swim in salty seas. Trust yourself. Trust the Power of the Water. Whether you dive into an ocean lit by the moon and the stars, or into a sun-burnished sea, swim with more than your arms and legs. Swim with all you are, reaching for horizons you have yet to see or to imagine.

How can I tell you all it means to swim?
To love each breath,
To lose yourself in the deepening water,
And, swimming, find your harbor—
Find your home.

SWIMMING PRACTICE

Swimming Lesson Ten:
Swimming in the Ocean

1. Write about whether you want to venture out into the ocean—the Off Somewhere. Use the prompt: "I choose (do not choose) to swim in the ocean because _____."

2. Make a list of the unconventional angels you've encountered in your life. Consider writing, calling, or otherwise communicating with those angels, if possible, to thank them for what they have done for you and for what they have meant to you.

3. Communicate your vision of a better world by listing, in order of importance, the five most significant positive changes you would like to see in your own country, in your own lifetime. Reflect on whether and how these changes might happen.

Next, list, in order of importance, the most significant positive changes you would like to see in the world, in your lifetime. Reflect on whether and how these changes might happen.

4. Give some thought to ways to put your voice and some of your life on paper, on film, on tape, in art—ways to say to the future, "I was here. This is what I saw and did and learned and felt. This is who I was."

Maybe you will write a journal or memoir, or compile a scrapbook or album of pictures, clippings, or other memorabilia. Maybe you'll create a series of audio or video recordings, or a visual memoir in the form of paintings, photographs, or handcrafts—such as a model of your family home place, a hand-stitched quilt, a wood carving. One grandmother I know filled small trunks with books and other keepsakes for each of her grandchildren. Maybe you will decide to create a time capsule, as suggested below.

5. On paper or with actual objects, create a personal time capsule with at least five items that reveal who you are and what matters to you. Write a brief note to explain the significance of each item. Then, with your family and/or friends, create a community time capsule, with the same purpose. Put these time capsules away, and get them out a year from now, five years from now, ten years from now. They will help you discover what has remained the same and what has changed as you swim toward Tomorrow.

Acknowledgments

THIS BOOK BEGAN as a journal—speculations, reflections, and meditations about swimming as a metaphor for living a life. Jennifer, my beloved daughter, was the first to say, "It sounds like a book to me." Accustomed as I am to digging deeply into other people's lives, I found it alternately intimidating and exhilarating to try to make some sense of my own.

When I first shared this idea with Barbara Hogenson, my friend as well as my literary agent, she urged me to defer some other projects to concentrate on this one. Then Kati Steele Hesford, senior editor of Harvest at Harcourt, took an interest in the book. She got it right away, saw my vision, and heard my voice. I owe debts I can't repay to these three fellow swimmers, Jennifer, Barbara, and Kati.

I send my thanks as well to Tim Jacobs, the patient teacher who got me into the Earlham College pool in Richmond, Indiana, and pushed me toward the deep water, telling me all the while I could swim. Thanks, too, to Jody Doll and other companions in the class, and to Joe Kraemer who accompanied Jennifer and me on many of our practice swims, stirring the waters with his inimitable, exuberant free style. I salute my swimming partners, Jane Silver and Caroline Richards, even though we've yet to achieve our dream of the perfect water ballet.

This book and I have been touched by the stories many other swimmers have shared. I am grateful to the people of Waxhaw, North Carolina. Frances Niven Gamble and Harry Yandle Gamble, my aunt and uncle (who live Off Somewhere, in Roanoke, Virginia), have given me love, laughter, and nurture all of my life, especially these last few years, when I have needed them most. My sister, Lynn Niven Duval Clark, has given this book and me enduring support, imbued with thoughtfulness and good cheer. I thank Doris Niven Knapp, my sister, and William Olin "Bill" Niven, my brother, for letting me share their stories.

I've been blessed by the friendship and steady encouragement of Claire Christopher, who read and listened to parts of the manuscript in progress, and made helpful and sensitive suggestions. My life and my work are deeply enriched by my writers' group—Ginger Hendricks, Joy Beshears Hagy, and Sheryl Stanley Monks—former students, fellow writers, and remarkable women. I will always appreciate composer Michael Hoppé's insights into the creative process, as well as his music, his encouragement, and his enthusiasm.

I appreciate Kati Hesford's astute editing, her perceptive questions, and her effervescent spirit. She is skilled and wise beyond her years. I thank all the people at Harcourt who have worked on this book, especially Kelly Eismann, Gayle Feallock, Linda Lockowitz, Elizabeth Royles Parker, and Tricia van Dockum, and illustrator Jim Nocito. Gratitude, affection, and esteem go out to Barbara Hogenson and Nicole Verity of The Barbara Hogenson Agency; Eileen Wilson-Oyelaran of Salem College; Coddy Granum; Robert Hamilton; Francesca Calderone-Steichen; James Earl and Cecilia Hart Jones; Helga Sandburg; Tappan Wilder; and my wonderful son-in-law, John Michael Hreno, III.

At the heart of everything is Jennifer: daughter, writer, swimmer, friend, and wondrous person beyond compare. I call her my finest work of art, all the while recognizing that her art, beauty, love, and grace pour out of her own luminous spirit.

And, always, I write in loving memory of my extraordinary parents, Olin and Eleanor Marsh Hearon Niven.